STORYTELLER

Also by Leslie Marmon Silko

LAGUNA WOMAN

CEREMONY

STORYTELLER
LESLIE MARMON SILKO

SEAVER BOOKS ❧ NEW YORK

First Edition 1981
First Printing 1981
ISBN: 0-394-51589-7 (hardbound)
        0-394-17795-9 (paperbound)
Seaver Books ISBN: 0-86579-004-3
Library of Congress Catalog Card Number: 80-20251

LIBRARY OF CONGRESS CATALOGING IN PUBLICATION DATA
Silko, Leslie, 1948-
Storyteller.
I. Title.
PS3569.I44S8   813′.54   80-20251
ISBN 0-394-51589-7 hdbk.
ISBN 0-394-17795-9 pbk.

Some of the material in this volume has appeared previ-
   ously in the following publications:
American Literature: Themes and Writers (third edition)
Chicago Review
Fiction's Journey: 50 Stories
Focus on America
Rocky Mountain Magazine
Series E, Macmillan English
Sight and Insight: Steps in the Writing Process
The Best American Short Stories 1975
The Ethnic American Woman: Problems, Protests, Lifestyle
The Man to Send Rain Clouds
The Remembered Earth: An Anthology of Contemporary
   Native American Literature
The Third Woman
200 Years of Great American Short Stories
Voices of the Rainbow

Manufactured in the United States of America
Distributed by Grove Press Inc., New York
SEAVER BOOKS, 333 Central Park West,
New York, N.Y.10025

This book is dedicated to the storytellers
as far back as memory goes and to the telling
which continues and through which they all live
and we with them.

ACKNOWLEDGMENT

Thank you, Mei-Mei, for your suggestions,
and thank you, Jim, for your beautiful letters,
and thank you, Beth, for your lovely design.
Jeannette Seaver, thank you for your patience
and faith in me.

ACKNOWLEDGMENT

Special thanks and my love to Denny
for helping me bring together
the stories and the photographs
which are themselves part of the stories.

STORYTELLER

There is a tall Hopi basket with a single figure
woven into it which might be a Grasshopper or
a Hummingbird Man. Inside the basket are hundreds
of photographs taken since the 1890's around Laguna.
My grandpa Hank first had a camera when he returned
from Indian School, and years later, my father learned
photography in the Army.

Photographs have always had special significance
with the people of my family and the people at Laguna.
A photograph is serious business and many people
still do not trust just anyone to take their picture.

It wasn't until I began this book
that I realized that the photographs in the Hopi basket
have a special relationship to the stories as I remember them.
The photographs are here because they are part of many of the stories
and because many of the stories can be traced in the photographs.

1

I always called her Aunt Susie
because she was my father's aunt
and that's what he called her.

She was married to Walter K. Marmon,
my grandpa Hank's brother.
Her family was the Reyes family from Paguate
the village north of Old Laguna.
Around 1896
when she was a young woman
she had been sent away to Carlisle Indian School
in Pennsylvania.
After she finished at the Indian School
she attended Dickinson College in Carlisle.

When she returned to Laguna
she continued her studies
particularly of history
even as she raised her family
and helped Uncle Walter run their small cattle ranch.
In the 1920's she taught school
in a one-room building at Old Laguna

where my father remembers he misbehaved
while Aunt Susie had her back turned.

From the time that I can remember her
she worked on her kitchen table
with her books and papers spread over the oil cloth.
She wrote beautiful long hand script
but her eyesight was not good
and so she wrote very slowly.

She was already in her mid-sixties
when I discovered that she would listen to me
to all my questions and speculations.
I was only seven or eight years old then
but I remember she would put down her fountain pen
and lift her glasses to wipe her eyes with her handkerchief
before she spoke.

It seems extraordinary now
that she took time from her studies and writing
to answer my questions
and to tell me all that she knew on a subject,
but she did.

She had come to believe very much in books
and in schooling.
She was of a generation,
the last generation here at Laguna,

2

that passed down an entire culture
by word of mouth
an entire history
an entire vision of the world
which depended upon memory
and retelling by subsequent generations.

She must have realized
that the atmosphere and conditions
which had maintained this oral tradition in Laguna culture
had been irrevocably altered by the European intrusion—
principally by the practice of taking the children
away from Laguna to Indian schools,
taking the children away from the tellers who had
in all past generations
told the children
an entire culture, an entire identity of a people.

And yet her writing went painfully slow
because of her failing eyesight
and because of her considerable family duties.
What she is leaving with us—
the stories and remembered accounts—
is primarily what she was able to tell
and what we are able to remember.

As with any generation
the oral tradition depends upon each person

listening and remembering a portion
and it is together—
all of us remembering what we have heard together—
that creates the whole story
the long story of the people.

I remember only a small part.
But this is what I remember.

꠵

This is the way Aunt Susie told the story.
She had certain phrases, certain distinctive words
she used in her telling.
I write when I still hear
her voice as she tells the story.
People are sometimes surprised
at her vocabulary, but she was
a brilliant woman, a scholar
of her own making
who has cherished the Laguna stories
all her life.
This is the way I remember
she told this one story
about the little girl who ran away.

7

The scene is laid partly in old Acoma, and Laguna.
Waithea was a little girl living in Acoma and
one day she said

    "Mother, I would like to have
    some *yashtoah* to eat."
"Yashtoah" is the hardened crust on corn meal mush
that curls up.
The very name "yashtoah" means
it's sort of curled-up, you know, dried,
just as mush dries on top.
She said

    "I would like to have some *yashtoah*,"
and her mother said

      "My dear little girl,
      I can't make you any *yashtoah*
      because we haven't any wood,
      but if you will go down off the mesa
      down below
      and pick up some pieces of wood
      bring them home
      and I will make you some *yashtoah*."
So Waithea was glad and ran down the precipitous cliff
of Acoma mesa.
Down below
just as her mother had told her
there were pieces of wood,
some curled, some crooked in shape,
that she was to pick up and take home.

8

She found just such wood as these.
She went home
and she had them
in a little wicker basket-like bag.

First she called her mother
as she got home.
She said
        "Nayah, deeni!
          mother, upstairs!"
The pueblo people always called "upstairs"
because long ago their homes were two, three stories high
and that was their entrance
from the top.
She said
        "Deeni!
          UPSTAIRS!"
and her mother came.
The little girl said
                "I have brought the wood
                    you wanted me to bring."
And she opened
her little wicker basket
and laid them out
and here they were snakes
instead of the crooked sticks of wood.
And her mother says

9

"Oh my dear child,
　　you have brought snakes instead!"
She says
　　"Go take them back and put them back
　　　just where you got them."
And the little girl
ran down the mesa again
down below in the flats
and she put those sticks back
just where she got them.
They were snakes instead
and she was very much hurt about this
and so she said
　　　"I'm not going home.
　　　I'm going to *Kawaik,*
　　　　the beautiful lake place, *Kawaik*
　　　　and drown myself
　　　　in that lake, *bun'yah'nah.*
That means the "west lake."
　　　　I'll go there and drown myself."
So she started off,
and as she came by the Enchanted Mesa
near Acoma
she met an old man very aged
and he saw her running and he says
　　　　"My dear child,
　　　　　where are you going?"
10　　She says

"I'm going to *Kawaik*
      and jump into the lake there."
"Why?"
"Well, because,"
          she says
"my mother didn't want to make any *yashtoah*
for me."
The old man said "Oh no!
      You must not go my child.
      Come with me
      and I will take you home."
He tried to catch her
but she was very light
and skipped along.
And everytime he would try
to grab her
she would skip faster
away from him.
So he was coming home with some wood
on his back,
strapped to his back
and tied with yucca thongs.
That's the way they did
in those days, with a strap
across their forehead.
And so he just took that strap
and let the wood drop.
He went as fast as he could

11

up the cliff
to the little girl's home.
When he got to the place
where she lived
he called to her mother
                    "Deeni!"
"Come on up!"
And he says
            "I can't.
            I just came to bring you a message.
            Your little daughter is running away,
            she's going to *Kawaik* to drown herself
            in the lake there."
"Oh my dear little girl!"
                    the mother said.
So she busied herself around
and made the *yashtoah* for her
which she liked so much.
Corn mush curled at the top.
She must have found enough wood
to boil the corn meal
to make the "yashtoah"
And while the mush was cooling off
she got the little girl's clothing
she got her little *manta* dress,
you know,
and all her other garments,
her little buckskin moccasins that she had

and put them in a bundle too,
probably a yucca bag,
and started down as fast as she could on the east side of Acoma.
There used to be a trail there, you know, it is gone now, but
it was accessible in those days.
And she followed
and she saw her way at a distance,
saw the daughter way at a distance.
She kept calling
        "*Stsamaku*! My daughter! Come back!
        I've got your *yashtoah* for you."
But the girl would not turn
she kept on ahead and she cried
               "My mother, my mother.
               She didn't want me to have any *yashtoah*
               so now I'm going to *Kawaik*
               and drown myself."
Her mother heard her cry
and says
       "My little daughter
       come back here!"
No, she kept a distance away from her
and they came nearer and nearer
to the lake that was here.
And she could see her daughter now
very plain.
       "Come back my daughter!
       I have your *yashtoah!*"

And no
she kept on
and finally she reached the lake
and she stood on the edge.

She had carried a little feather
which is traditional.
In death they put this feather
on the dead in the hair.
She carried a feather
the little girl did
and she tied it in her hair
with a little piece of string
right on top of her head
she put the feather.
Just as her mother was about
to reach her
she jumped
into the lake.

The little feather was whirling
around and around in the depths below.
Of course the mother was very sad.
She went, grieved back to Acoma
and climbed her mesa home.
And the little clothing,
the little moccasins
that she's brought

and the *yashtoah,*
she stood on the edge
of the high mesa
and scattered them out.
She scattered them to the east
                    to the west
to the north and to the south—
in all directions—
and here every one of the little clothing—
            the little *manta* dresses and shawls
            the moccasins and the *yashtoah*—
            they all turned into butterflies—
            all colors of butterflies.
And today they say that acoma has more beautiful butterflies—
red ones, white ones, blue ones, yellow ones.
They came
from this little girl's clothing.

Aunt Susie always spoke the words of the mother to her daughter
with great tenderness, with great feeling
as if Aunt Susie herself were the mother
addressing her little child. I remember there was something mournful
in her voice too as she repeated the words of the old man
something in her voice that implied the tragedy to come.
But when Aunt Susie came to the place
where the little girl's clothes turned into butterflies
then her voice would change and I could hear the excitement and wonder
and the story wasn't sad any longer.

15

My great-grandmother was Marie Anaya
from Paguate village north of Old Laguna.
She had married my great-grandfather, Robert G. Marmon,
after her sister, who had been married to him,
died. There were two small children then,
and she married him so the children would have a mother.
She had been sent East
to the Indian school at Carlisle
and she later made a trip
with the children to Ohio
where my great-grandpa's relatives, the Marmons, lived.
My great-grandpa didn't go with them and
he never seemed much interested in returning to Ohio.
He had learned to speak Laguna
and Grandpa Hank said when great-grandpa went away from Laguna
white people who knew
sometimes called him "Squaw Man."

Grandpa Hank and his brother Kenneth
were just little boys
when my great-grandfather took them
on one of his trips to Albuquerque.

The boys got hungry
so great-grandpa started to take them
through the lobby of the only hotel in Albuquerque
at that time.
Grandpa Hank said that when the hotel manager
spotted him and Kenneth
the manager stopped them.
He told Grandpa Marmon that he was always welcome
when he was alone
but when he had Indians with him
he should use the back entrance to reach the café.
My great-grandfather said,
                    "These are my sons."
He walked out of the hotel
and never would set foot in that hotel again
not even years later
when they began to allow Indians inside.

STORYTELLER

Every day the sun came up a little lower on the horizon, moving more slowly until one day she got excited and started calling the jailer. She realized she had been sitting there for many hours, yet the sun had not moved from the center of the sky. The color of the sky had not been good lately; it had been pale blue, almost white, even when there were no clouds. She told herself it wasn't a good sign for the sky to be indistinguishable from the river ice, frozen solid and white against the earth. The tundra rose up behind the river but all the boundaries between the river and hills and sky were lost in the density of the pale ice.

She yelled again, this time some English words which came randomly into her mouth, probably swear words she'd heard from the oil drilling crews last winter. The jailer was an Eskimo, but he would not speak Yupik to her. She had watched people in other cells, when they spoke to him in Yupik he ignored them until they spoke English.

He came and stared at her. She didn't know if he understood what she was telling him until he glanced behind her at the small high window. He looked at the sun, and turned and walked away. She could hear the buckles on his heavy snowmobile boots jingle as he walked to the front of the building.

It was like the other buildings that white people, the Gussucks, brought with them: BIA and school buildings, portable buildings that arrived sliced in halves, on barges coming up the river. Squares of metal panelling bulged out with the layers of insulation stuffed inside. She had asked once what it was and someone told her it was to keep out the cold. She had not laughed then, but she did now. She walked over to the small double-pane window and she laughed out loud. They thought they could keep out the cold with stringy yellow wadding. Look at the sun. It wasn't moving; it was frozen, caught in the middle of the sky. Look at the sky, solid as the river with ice which had trapped the sun. It had not moved for a long time; in a few more hours it would be weak, and heavy frost would begin to appear on the edges and spread across the face of the sun like a mask. Its light was pale yellow, worn thin by the winter.

She could see people walking down the snow-packed roads, their breath steaming out from their parka hoods, faces hidden and protected by deep ruffs of fur. There were no cars or snowmobiles that day; the cold had silenced their machines. The metal froze; it split and shattered. Oil hardened and moving parts jammed solidly. She had seen it happen to their big yellow machines and the giant drill last winter when they came to drill their test holes. The cold stopped them, and they were helpless against it.

Her village was many miles upriver from this town, but in her mind she could see it clearly. Their house was not near the village houses. It stood alone on the bank upriver from the village. Snow had drifted to the eaves of the roof on the north side, but on the west side, by the door, the path was almost clear. She had nailed scraps of red tin over the logs last summer. She had done it for the bright red color, not for added warmth the way the village people had done. This final winter had been coming even then; there had been signs of its approach for many years.

She went because she was curious about the big school where the Government sent all the other girls and boys. She had not played much with the village children while she was growing up because they were afraid of the old man, and they ran when her grandmother came. She went because she was tired of being alone with the old woman whose body had been stiffening for as long as the girl could remember. Her knees and knuckles were swollen grotesquely, and the pain had squeezed the brown skin of her face tight against the bones; it left her eyes hard like river stone. The girl asked once what it was that did this to her body, and the old woman had raised up from sewing a sealskin boot, and stared at her.

"The joints," the old woman said in a low voice, whispering like wind across the roof, "the joints are swollen with anger."

Sometimes she did not answer and only stared at the girl. Each year she spoke less and less, but the old man talked more—all night sometimes, not to anyone but himself; in a soft deliberate voice, he told stories, moving his smooth brown hands above the blankets. He had not fished or hunted with the other men for many years, although he was not crippled or sick. He stayed in his bed, smelling like dry fish and urine, telling stories all winter; and when warm weather came, he went to his place on the river bank. He sat with a long willow stick, poking at the smoldering moss he burned against the insects while he continued with the stories.

The trouble was that she had not recognized the warnings in time. She did not see what the Gussuck school would do to her until she walked into the dormitory and realized that the old man had not been lying about the place. She thought he had been trying to scare her as he used to when she was very small and her grandmother was outside cutting up fish. She hadn't believed what he told her about the school because she knew he wanted to keep her there in the log house with him. She knew what he wanted.

The dormitory matron pulled down her underpants and whipped her with a leather belt because she refused to speak English.

"Those backwards village people," the matron

19

said, because she was an Eskimo who had worked for the BIA a long time, "they kept this one until she was too big to learn." The other girls whispered in English. They knew how to work the showers, and they washed and curled their hair at night. They ate Gussuck food. She lay on her bed and imagined what her grandmother might be sewing, and what the old man was eating in his bed. When summer came, they sent her home.

The way her grandmother had hugged her before she left for school had been a warning too, because the old woman had not hugged or touched her for many years. Not like the old man, whose hands were always hunting, like ravens circling lazily in the sky, ready to touch her. She was not surprised when the priest and the old man met her at the landing strip, to say that the old lady was gone. The priest asked her where she would like to stay. He referred to the old man as her grandfather, but she did not bother to correct him. She had already been thinking about it; if she went with the priest, he would send her away to a school. But the old man was different. She knew he wouldn't send her back to school. She knew he wanted to keep her.

He told her one time, that she would get too old for him faster than he got too old for her; but again she had not believed him because sometimes he lied. He had lied about what he would do with her if she came into his bed. But as the years passed, she realized what he said was true. She was restless and strong. She had no patience with the old man who had never changed his slow smooth motions under the blankets.

The old man was in his bed for the winter; he did not leave it except to use the slop bucket in the corner. He was dozing with his mouth open slightly; his lips quivered and sometimes they moved like he was telling a story even while he dreamed. She pulled on the sealskin boots, the mukluks with the bright red flannel linings her grandmother had sewn for her, and she tied the braided red yarn tassels around her ankles over the gray wool pants. She zipped the wolfskin parka. Her grandmother had worn it for many years, but the old man said that before she died, she instructed him to bury her in an old black sweater, and to give the parka to the girl. The wolf pelts were creamy colored and silver, almost white in some places, and when the old lady had walked across the tundra in the winter, she was invisible in the snow.

She walked toward the village, breaking her

own path through the deep snow. A team of sled dogs tied outside a house at the edge of the village leaped against their chains to bark at her. She kept walking, watching the dusky sky for the first evening stars. It was warm and the dogs were alert. When it got cold again, the dogs would lie curled and still, too drowsy from the cold to bark or pull at the chains. She laughed loudly because it made them howl and snarl. Once the old man had seen her tease the dogs and he shook his head. "So that's the kind of woman you are," he said, "in the wintertime the two of us are no different from those dogs. We wait in the cold for someone to bring us a few dry fish."

She laughed out loud again, and kept walking. She was thinking about the Gussuck oil drillers. They were strange; they watched her when she walked near their machines. She wondered what they looked like underneath their quilted goose-down trousers; she wanted to know how they moved. They would be something different from the old man.

The old man screamed at her. He shook her shoulders so violently that her head bumped against the log wall. "I smelled it!" he yelled, "as soon as I woke up! I am sure of it now. You can't fool me!" His thin legs were shaking inside the baggy wool trousers; he stumbled over her boots in his bare feet. His toenails were long and yellow like bird claws; she had seen a gray crane last summer fighting another in the shallow water on the edge of the river. She laughed out loud and pulled her shoulder out of his grip. He stood in front of her. He was breathing hard and shaking; he looked weak. He would probably die next winter.

"I'm warning you," he said, "I'm warning you." He crawled back into his bunk then, and reached under the old soiled feather pillow for a piece of dry fish. He lay back on the pillow, staring at the ceiling and chewed dry strips of salmon. "I don't know what the old woman told you," he said, "but there will be trouble." He looked over to see if she was listening. His face suddenly relaxed into a smile, his dark slanty eyes were lost in wrinkles of brown skin. "I could tell you, but you are too good for warnings now. I can smell what you did all night with the Gussucks."

She did not understand why they came there, because the village was small and so far upriver that even some Eskimos who had been away to school did not want to come back. They stayed downriver in the town. They said the village was too quiet. They were used to the town where the boarding school was located, with electric lights and running water. After all those years away at school, they had forgotten how to set nets in the river and where to hunt seals in the fall. When she asked the old man why the Gussucks bothered to come to the village, his narrow eyes got bright with excitement.

"They only come when there is something to steal. The fur animals are too difficult for them to get now, and the seals and fish are hard to find. Now they come for oil deep in the earth. But this is the last time for them." His breathing was wheezy and fast; his hands gestured at the sky. "It is approaching. As it comes, ice will push across the sky." His eyes were open wide and he stared at the low ceiling rafters for hours without blinking. She remembered all this clearly because he began the story that day, the story he told from that time on. It began with a giant bear which he described muscle by muscle, from the curve of the ivory claws to the whorls of hair at the top of the massive skull. And for eight days he did not sleep, but talked continuously of the giant bear whose color was pale blue glacier ice.

The snow was dirty and worn down in a path to the door. On either side of the path, the snow was higher than her head. In front of the door there were jagged yellow stains melted into the snow where men had urinated. She stopped in the entry way and kicked the snow off her boots. The room was dim; a kerosene lantern by the cash register was burning low. The long wooden shelves were jammed with cans of beans and potted meats. On the bottom shelf a jar of mayonnaise was broken open, leaking oily white clots on the floor. There was no one in the room except the yellowish dog sleeping in the front of the long glass display case. A reflection made it appear to be lying on the knives and ammunition inside the case. Gussucks kept dogs inside their houses with them; they did not seem to mind the odors which seeped out of the dogs. "They tell us we are dirty for the food we eat—raw fish and fermented meat. But we do not live with dogs," the old man once said. She heard voices in the back room, and the sound of bottles set down hard on tables.

They were always confident. The first year they waited for the ice to break up on the river, and then they brought their big yellow machines up river on barges. They planned to drill their test holes during the summer to avoid the freezing. But the imprints and graves of their machines were still there, on the edge of the tundra above the river, where the summer mud had swallowed them before they ever left sight of the river. The village people had gathered to watch the white men, and to laugh as they drove the giant machines, one by one, off the steel ramp into the bogs; as if sheer numbers of vehicles would somehow make the tundra solid. But the old man said they behaved like desperate people, and they would come back again. When the tundra was frozen solid, they returned.

Village women did not even look through the door to the back room. The priest had warned them. The storeman was watching her because he didn't let Eskimos or Indians sit down at the tables in the back room. But she knew he couldn't throw her out if one of his Gussuck customers invited her to sit with him. She walked across the room. They stared at her, but she had the feeling she was walking for someone else, not herself, so their eyes did not matter. The red-haired man pulled out a chair and motioned for her to sit down. She looked back at the storeman while the red-haired man poured her a glass of red sweet wine. She wanted to laugh at the storeman the way she laughed at the dogs, straining against the chains, howling at her.

The red-haired man kept talking to the other Gussucks sitting around the table, but he slid one hand off the top of the table to her thigh. She looked over at the storeman to see if he was still watching her. She laughed out loud at him and the red-haired man stopped talking and turned to her. He asked if she wanted to go. She nodded and stood up.

Someone in the village had been telling him things about her, he said as they walked down the road to his trailer. She understood that much of what he was saying, but the rest she did not hear. The whine of the big generators at the construction camp sucked away the sound of his words. But English was of no concern to her anymore, and neither was anything the Christians in the village might say about her or the old man. She smiled at the effect of the subzero air on the electric lights around the trailers; they did not shine. They left only flat yellow holes in the darkness.

It took him a long time to get ready, even after she had undressed for him. She waited in the bed with the blankets pulled close, watching him. He adjusted the thermostat and lit candles in the room, turning out the electric lights. He searched through a stack of record albums until he found the right one. She was not sure about the last thing he did: he taped something on the wall behind the bed where he could see it while he lay on top of her. He was shriveled and white from the cold; he pushed against her body for warmth. He guided her hands to his thighs; he was shivering.

She had returned a last time because she wanted to know what it was he stuck on the wall above the bed. After he finished each time, he reached up and pulled it loose, folding it carefully so that she could not see it. But this time she was ready; she waited for his fast breathing and sudden collapse on top of her. She slid out from under him and stood up beside the bed. She looked at the picture while she got dressed. He did not raise his face from the pillow, and she thought she heard teeth rattling together as she left the room.

She heard the old man move when she came in. After the Gussuck's trailer, the log house felt cool. It smelled like dry fish and cured meat. The room was dark except for the blinking yellow flame in the mica window of the oil stove. She squatted in front of the stove and watched the flames for a long time before she walked to the bed where her grandmother had slept. The bed was covered with a mound of rags and fur scraps the old woman had saved. She reached into the mound until she felt something cold and solid wrapped in a wool blanket. She pushed her fingers around it until she felt smooth stone. Long ago, before the Gussucks came, they had burned whale oil in the big stone lamp which made light and heat as well. The old woman had saved everything they would need when the time came.

In the morning, the old man pulled a piece of dry caribou meat from under the blankets and offered it to her. While she was gone, men from the village had brought a bundle of dry meat. She chewed it slowly, thinking about the way they still came from the village to take care of the old man and his stories. But she had a story now, about the red-haired Gussuck. The old man knew what she was thinking, and his smile made his face seem more round than it was.

"Well," he said, "what was it?"

"A woman with a big dog on top of her."

He laughed softly to himself and walked over to the water barrel. He dipped the tin cup into the water.

"It doesn't surprise me," he said.

"Grandma," she said, "there was something red in the grass that morning. I remember." She had not asked about her parents before. The old woman stopped splitting the fish bellies open for the willow drying racks. Her jaw muscles pulled so tightly against her skull, the girl thought the old woman would not be able to speak.

"They bought a tin can full of it from the storeman. Late at night. He told them it was alcohol safe to drink. They traded a rifle for it." The old woman's voice sounded like each word stole strength from her. "It made no difference about the rifle. That year the Gussuck boats had come, firing big guns at the walrus and seals. There was nothing left to hunt after that anyway. So," the old lady said, in a low soft voice the girl had not heard for a long time, "I didn't say anything to them when they left that night."

"Right over there," she said, pointing at the fallen poles, half buried in the river sand and tall grass, "in the summer shelter. The sun was high half the night then. Early in the morning when it was still low, the policeman came around. I told the interpreter to tell him that the storeman had poisoned them." She made outlines in the air in front of her, showing how their bodies lay twisted on the sand; telling the story was like laboring to walk through deep snow; sweat shone in the white hair around her forehead. "I told the priest too, after he came. I told him the storeman lied."

She turned away from the girl. She held her mouth even tighter, set solidly, not in sorrow or anger, but against the pain, which was all that remained. "I never believed," she said, "not much anyway. I wasn't surprised when the priest did nothing."

The wind came off the river and folded the tall grass into itself like river waves. She could feel the silence the story left, and she wanted to have the old woman go on.

"I heard sounds that night, grandma. Sounds like someone was singing. It was light outside. I could see something red on the ground." The old woman did not answer her; she moved to the tub full of fish on the ground beside the workbench. She stabbed her knife into the belly of a whitefish and lifted it onto the bench. "The Gussuck storeman left the village right after that," the old woman said as she pulled the entrails from the fish, "otherwise, I could tell you more." The old woman's voice flowed with the wind blowing off the river; they never spoke of it again.

When the willows got their leaves and the grass grew tall along the river banks and around the sloughs, she walked early in the morning. While the sun was still low on the horizon, she listened to the wind off the river; its sound was like the voice that day long ago. In the distance,

25

she could hear the engines of the machinery the oil drillers had left the winter before, but she did not go near the village or the store. The sun never left the sky and the summer became the same long day, with only the winds to fan the sun into brightness or allow it to slip into twilight.

She sat beside the old man at his place on the river bank. She poked the smoky fire for him, and felt herself growing wide and thin in the sun as if she had been split from belly to throat and strung on the willow pole in preparation for the winter to come. The old man did not speak anymore. When men from the village brought him fresh fish he hid them deep in the river grass where it was cool. After he went inside, she split the fish open and spread them to dry on the willow frame the way the old woman had done. Inside, he dozed and talked to himself. He had talked all winter, softly and incessantly, about the giant polar bear stalking a lone hunter across Bering Sea ice. After all the months the old man had been telling the story, the bear was within a hundred feet of the man; but the ice fog had closed in on them now and the man could only smell the sharp ammonia odor of the bear, and hear the edge of the snow crust crack under the giant paws.

One night she listened to the old man tell the story all night in his sleep, describing each crystal of ice and the slightly different sounds they made under each paw; first the left and then the right paw, then the hind feet. Her grandmother was there suddenly, a shadow around the stove. She spoke in her low wind voice and the girl was afraid to sit up to hear more clearly. Maybe what she said had been to the old man because he stopped telling the story and began to snore softly the way he had long ago when the old woman had scolded him for telling his stories while others in the house were trying to sleep. But the last words she heard clearly: "It will take a long time, but the story must be told. There must not be any lies." She pulled the blankets up around her chin, slowly, so that her movements would not be seen. She thought her grandmother was talking about the old man's bear story; she did not know about the other story then.

She left the old man wheezing and snoring in his bed. She walked through river grass glistening with frost; the bright green summer color was already fading. She watched the sun move across the sky, already lower on the horizon, already moving away from the village. She stopped by the fallen poles of the summer shelter where her parents had died. Frost glittered on the river sand too; in a few more weeks there would be snow.

The predawn light would be the color of an old woman. An old woman sky full of snow. There had been something red lying on the ground the morning they died. She looked for it again, pushing aside the grass with her foot. She knelt in the sand and looked under the fallen structure for some trace of it. When she found it, she would know what the old woman had never told her. She squatted down close to the gray poles and leaned her back against them. The wind made her shiver.

The summer rain had washed the mud from between the logs; the sod blocks stacked as high as her belly next to the log walls had lost their square-cut shape and had grown into soft mounds of tundra moss and stiff-bladed grass bending with clusters of seed bristles. She looked at the northwest, in the direction of the Bering Sea. The cold would come down from there to find narrow slits in the mud, rainwater holes in the outer layer of sod which protected the log house. The dark green tundra stretched away flat and continuous. Somewhere the sea and the land met; she knew by their dark green colors there were no boundaries between them. That was how the cold would come: when the boundaries were gone the polar ice would range across the land into the sky. She watched the horizon for a long time. She would stand in that place on the north side of the house and she would keep watch on the northwest horizon, and eventually she would see it come. She would watch for its approach in the stars, and hear it come with the wind. These preparations were unfamiliar, but gradually she recognized them as she did her own footprints in the snow.

She emptied the slop jar beside his bed twice a day and kept the barrel full of water melted from river ice. He did not recognize her anymore, and when he spoke to her, he called her by her grandmother's name and talked about people and events from long ago, before he went back to telling the story. The giant bear was creeping across the new snow on its belly, close enough now that the man could hear the rasp of its breathing. On and on in a soft singing voice, the old man caressed the story, repeating the words again and again like gentle strokes.

The sky was gray like a river crane's egg; its density curved into the thin crust of frost already covering the land. She looked at the bright red color of the tin against the ground and the sky and she told the village men to bring the pieces for the old man and her. To drill the test holes in

27

the tundra, the Gussucks had used hundreds of barrels of fuel. The village people split open the empty barrels that were abandoned on the river bank, and pounded the red tin into flat sheets. The village people were using the strips of tin to mend walls and roofs for winter. But she nailed it on the log walls for its color. When she finished, she walked away with the hammer in her hand, not turning around until she was far away, on the ridge above the river banks, and then she looked back. She felt a chill when she saw how the sky and the land were already losing their boundaries, already becoming lost in each other. But the red tin penetrated the thick white color of earth and sky; it defined the boundaries like a wound revealing the ribs and heart of a great caribou about to bolt and be lost to the hunter forever. That night the wind howled and when she scratched a hole through the heavy frost on the inside of the window, she could see nothing but the impenetrable white; whether it was blowing snow or snow that had drifted as high as the house, she did not know.

It had come down suddenly, and she stood with her back to the wind looking at the river, its smoky water clotted with ice. The wind had blown the snow over the frozen river, hiding thin blue streaks where fast water ran under ice trans-

lucent and fragile as memory. But she could see shadows of boundaries, outlines of paths which were slender branches of solidity reaching out from the earth. She spent days walking on the river, watching the colors of ice that would safely hold her, kicking the heel of her boot into the snow crust, listening for a solid sound. When she could feel the paths through the soles of her feet, she went to the middle of the river where the fast gray water churned under a thin pane of ice. She looked back. On the river bank in the distance she could see the red tin nailed to the log house, something not swallowed up by the heavy white belly of the sky or caught in the folds of the frozen earth. It was time.

The wolverine fur around the hood of her parka was white with the frost from her breathing. The warmth inside the store melted it, and she felt tiny drops of water on her face. The storeman came in from the back room. She unzipped the parka and stood by the oil stove. She didn't look at him, but stared instead at the yellowish dog, covered with scabs of matted hair, sleeping in front of the stove. She thought of the Gussuck's picture, taped on the wall above the bed and she laughed out loud. The sound of her laughter was piercing; the yellow dog jumped to its feet and the hair bristled down its back. The storeman was watching her. She wanted to laugh again because he didn't know about the ice. He did not know that it was prowling the earth, or that it had already pushed its way into the sky to seize the sun. She sat down in the chair by the stove and shook her long hair loose. He was like a dog tied up all winter, watching while the others got fed. He remembered how she had gone with the oil drillers, and his blue eyes moved like flies crawling over her body. He held his thin pale lips like he wanted to spit on her. He hated the people because they had something of value, the old man said, something which the Gussucks could never have. They thought they could take it, suck it out of the earth or cut it from the mountains; but they were fools.

There was a matted hunk of dog hair on the floor by her foot. She thought of the yellow insulation coming unstuffed: their defense against the freezing going to pieces as it advanced on them. The ice was crouching on the northwest horizon like the old man's bear. She laughed out loud again. The sun would be down now; it was time.

The first time he spoke to her, she did not hear what he said, so she did not answer or even look up at him. He spoke to her again but his words were only noises coming from his pale mouth, trembling now as his anger began to unravel. He jerked her up and the chair fell over behind her. His arms were shaking and she could feel his hands tense up, pulling the edges of the parka tighter. He raised his fist to hit her, his thin body quivering with rage; but the fist collapsed with the desire he had for the valuable things, which, the old man had rightly said, was the only reason they came. She could hear his heart pounding as he held her close and arched his hips against her, groaning and breathing in spasms. She twisted away from him and ducked under his arms.

She ran with a mitten over her mouth, breathing through the fur to protect her lungs from the freezing air. She could hear him running behind her, his heavy breathing, the occasional sound of metal jingling against metal. But he ran without his parka or mittens, breathing the frozen air; its fire squeezed the lungs against the ribs and it was enough that he could not catch her near his store. On the river bank he realized how far he was from his stove, and the wads of yellow stuffing that held off the cold. But the girl was not able to run very fast through the deep drifts at the edge of the river. The twilight was luminous

29

and he could still see clearly for a long distance; he knew he could catch her so he kept running.

When she neared the middle of the river she looked over her shoulder. He was not following her tracks; he went straight across the ice, running the shortest distance to reach her. He was close then; his face was twisted and scarlet from the exertion and the cold. There was satisfaction in his eyes; he was sure he could outrun her.

She was familiar with the river, down to the instant ice flexed into hairline fractures, and the cracking bone-sliver sounds gathered momentum with the opening ice until the churning gray water was set free. She stopped and turned to the sound of the river and the rattle of swirling ice fragments where he fell through. She pulled off a mitten and zipped the parka to her throat. She was conscious then of her own rapid breathing.

She moved slowly, kicking the ice ahead with the heel of her boot, feeling for sinews of ice to hold her. She looked ahead and all around herself; in the twilight, the dense white sky had merged into the flat snow-covered tundra. In the frantic running she had lost her place on the river. She stood still. The east bank of the river was lost in the sky; the boundaries had been swallowed by the freezing white. But then, in the distance, she saw something red, and suddenly it was as she had remembered it all those years.

She sat on her bed and while she waited, she listened to the old man. The hunter had found a small jagged knoll on the ice. He pulled his beaver fur cap off his head; the fur inside it steamed with his body heat and sweat. He left it upside down on the ice for the great bear to stalk, and he waited downwind on top of the ice knoll; he was holding the jade knife.

She thought she could see the end of his story in the way he wheezed out the words; but still he reached into his cache of dry fish and dribbled water into his mouth from the tin cup. All night she listened to him describe each breath the man took, each motion of the bear's head as it tried to catch the sound of the man's breathing, and tested the wind for his scent.

The state trooper asked her questions, and the woman who cleaned house for the priest translated them into Yupik. They wanted to know what happened to the storeman, the Gussuck who had been seen running after her down the road onto the river late last evening. He had not come back, and the Gussuck boss in Anchorage was concerned about him. She did not answer for a long time because the old man suddenly sat up in his bed and began to talk excitedly, looking at all of them—the trooper in his dark glasses and the housekeeper in her corduroy parka. He kept saying, "The story! The story! Eh-ya! The great bear! The hunter!"

They asked her again, what happened to the man from the Northern Commercial store. "He lied to them. He told them it was safe to drink. But I will not lie." She stood up and put on the gray wolfskin parka. "I killed him," she said, "but I don't lie."

The attorney came back again, and the jailer slid open the steel doors and opened the cell to let him in. He motioned for the jailer to stay to translate for him. She laughed when she saw how the jailer would be forced by this Gussuck to speak Yupik to her. She liked the Gussuck attorney for that, and for the thinning hair on his head. He was very tall, and she liked to think about the exposure of his head to the freezing; she wondered if he would feel the ice descending from the sky before the others did. He wanted to know why she told the state trooper she had killed the storeman. Some village children had seen it happen, he said, and it was an accident. "That's all you have to say to the judge: it was an accident." He kept repeating it over and over again to her, slowly in a loud but gentle voice: "It was an accident. He was running after you and he fell through the ice. That's all you have to say in court. That's all. And they will let you go home. Back to your village." The jailer translated the words sullenly, staring down at the floor. She shook her head. "I will not change the story, not even to escape this place and go home. I intended that he die. The story must be told as it is." The attorney exhaled loudly; his eyes looked tired. "Tell her that she could not have killed him that way. He was a white man. He ran after her without a parka or mittens. She could not have planned that." He paused and turned toward the cell door. "Tell her I will do all I can for her. I will explain to the judge that her mind is confused." She laughed out loud when the jailer translated what the attorney said. The Gussucks did not understand the story; they could not see the way it must be told, year after year as the old man had done, without lapse or silence.

She looked out the window at the frozen white sky. The sun had finally broken loose from the ice but it moved like a wounded caribou running on strength which only dying animals find, leaping and running on bullet-shattered lungs. Its light was weak and pale; it pushed dimly through the clouds. She turned and faced the Gussuck attorney.

"It began a long time ago," she intoned steadily, "in the summertime. Early in the morning, I remember, something red in the tall river grass. . . ."

The day after the old man died, men from the village came. She was sitting on the edge of her bed, across from the woman the trooper hired to watch her. They came into the room slowly and listened to her. At the foot of her bed they left a king salmon that had been slit open wide and dried last summer. But she did not pause or hesitate; she went on with the story, and she never stopped, not even when the woman got up to close the door behind the village men.

The old man would not change the story even when he knew the end was approaching. Lies could not stop what was coming. He thrashed around on the bed, pulling the blankets loose, knocking bundles of dried fish and meat on the floor. The hunter had been on the ice for many hours. The freezing winds on the ice knoll had numbed his hands in the mittens, and the cold had exhausted him. He felt a single muscle tremor in his hand that he could not stop, and the jade knife fell; it shattered on the ice, and the blue glacier bear turned slowly to face him.

❀

It was a long time before
I learned that my Grandma A'mooh's
real name was Marie Anaya Marmon.
I thought her name really was "A'mooh."
I realize now it had happened when I was a baby
and she cared for me while my mother worked.

I had been hearing her say
          "a'moo'ooh"
which is the Laguna expression of endearment
for a young child
spoken with great feeling and love.

Her house was next to ours
and as I grew up
I spent a lot of time with her
because she was in her eighties
and they worried about her falling.
So I would go check up on her—which was really
an excuse to visit her.
After I had to go to school
I went to carry in the coal bucket
which she still insisted on filling.
I slept with her
in case she fell getting up in the night.

She still washed her hair with yucca roots
or "soap weed" as she called it. She said
it kept white hair like hers from yellowing.
She kept these yucca roots on her windowsill
and I remember I was afraid of them for a long time
because they looked like hairy twisted claws.

I watched her make red chili on the grinding stone
the old way, even though it had gotten difficult for her

to get down on her knees.
She used to tell me and my sisters
about the old days when they didn't have toothpaste
and cleaned their teeth with juniper ash,
and how, instead of corn flakes, in the old days they ate
"*maaht'zini*" crushed up with milk poured over it.

Her last years they took her away to Albuquerque
to live with her daughter, Aunt Bessie.
But there was no fire to start in the morning
and nobody dropping by.
She didn't have anyone to talk to all day
because Bessie worked.
She might have lived without watering morning glories
and without kids running through her kitchen
but she did not last long
without someone to talk to.

INDIAN SONG: SURVIVAL

We went north
        to escape winter
climbing pale cliffs
            we paused   to sleep at the river.

Cold water   river cold from the north
I sink my body in the shallow
                   sink into sand and cold river water.

You sleep in the branches of
                 pale river willows above me.
I smell you in the silver leaves, mountain lion man
                   green willows aren't sweet enough to hide you.

I have slept with the river   and
                  he is warmer than any man.
At sunrise
       I heard ice on the cattails.

Mountain lion, with dark yellow eyes
                   you nibble moonflowers
                   while we wait.
I don't ask why do you come
                 on this desperation journey north.

I am hunted for my feathers
I hide in spider's web
             hanging   in a thin gray tree
                   above the river.
In the night   I hear music
             song of branches   dry leaves scraping the moon.

Green spotted frogs sing to the river
                and I know he is waiting.
Mountain lion shows me the way
           path of mountain wind
           climbing higher
                up
                  up to Cloudy Mountain.

It is only a matter of time, Indian
                you can't sleep with the river forever.
Smell winter and know.

I swallow black mountain dirt
          while you catch hummingbirds
            trap them with wildflowers
          pollen and petals
              fallen from the Milky Way.

You lie beside me in the sunlight
          warmth around us and
          you ask me if I still smell winter.
Mountain forest wind travels east and I answer:
           taste me,
              I am the wind
           touch me,
              I am the lean gray deer
          running on the edge of the rainbow.

The Laguna people
always begin their stories
with "humma-hah":
that means "long ago."
And the ones who are listening
say "aaaa-eh"

This story took place
somewhere around Acoma
where there was a lake,
a lake with pebbles along the edges.
It was a beautiful lake
and so a little girl and her sister
went there one day.
The older girl never liked to take care of her sister
but this day
she seemed to be anxious to take care of her sister.
So she put the little sister
on her back
That was the traditional way
of carrying babies, you know,
strapped on their back–

And so they went off to this lake
and this lake had shells around it

and butterflies and beautiful flowers—
they called it Shell Lake
shells and other pretty pebbles
where she amused her little sister
all day long.
And finally
toward evening
they came home to their village home.
And all was quiet in the village
there seemed to be no one stirring around or left,
and then
when they got to their house
which was a two-story house
traditional home of the Keres
she called *"Deeni!* Upstairs!"
because the entrance was generally from the top.

No one answered
until an old man came out
decrepit and he says
"You poor children—
nobody is here.
All our people have gone to Maúhuatl."
That was the name
of the high place
where they all went that day
to escape the flood that was coming.

He says
"Today the earth is going to be
filled with water.
And everyone has gone
to Maúhuatl
that high mesa land
to escape drowning.
Your mother is not here.
She left early in the day
to go with the rest of the people.
Only the old people
who cannot travel
are left.
And if you and your little sister
follow the rest
you can tell by their foot tracks.
But be sure and walk fast—
make haste
because the flood may be coming up
before you reach the mesa."

So she said they would.
She started off with her little sister on her back and
pretty soon they began to cry
and what they cried
is a song that is sung.
Their crying became this little song.
It goes like this:

Little sister go to sleep, go to sleep.
I suppose our mother didn't think much
of us
so she left us behind. Go to sleep. Go to sleep.
By luck we might catch up to the crowd. Go to sleep.
We might catch up to our mother who has gone
ahead to Maúhuatl. Go to sleep.

That is how the song goes.
And so the little girl kept walking
faster and faster.
By that time
the water was coming up to her ankles.
She was wading along
and as they went along
her little sister on her back
began to cry again.
She sang
       Go to sleep little sister, go to sleep.
       I suppose our mother didn't think much of us
       Or she wouldn't have left us behind.
By that time
the water had come up her legs
almost to her knees
and finally they reached the bottom
of Maúhuatl which was a mesa.
And there was a trail up there
and finally the older girl

walked up the mesa steps—
stone formations like steps.
They got to the top
before the flood really reached the top
and they looked around and
saw the people—
all the people up there
who had gone before.
They looked around
but they didn't see anything
of their mother.
They sat down,
the older girl did.
She saw the rest of them sitting around
holding their babies
and holding their little ones on their laps
so she thought she would sit down too
and hold her little sister on her lap.
Which she did.
She sat there for a little while
and then they all turned into stone.

The story ends there.
Some of the stories
Aunt Susie told
have this kind of ending.
There are no explanations.

LULLABY

The sun had gone down but the snow in the wind gave off its own light. It came in thick tufts like new wool—washed before the weaver spins it. Ayah reached out for it like her own babies had, and she smiled when she remembered how she had laughed at them. She was an old woman now, and her life had become memories. She sat down with her back against the wide cottonwood tree, feeling the rough bark on her back bones; she faced east and listened to the wind and snow sing a high-pitched Yeibechei song. Out of the wind she felt warmer, and she could watch the wide fluffy snow fill in her tracks, steadily, until the direction she had come from was gone. By the light of the snow she could see the dark outline of the big arroyo a few feet away. She was sitting on the edge of Cebolleta Creek, where in the springtime the thin cows would graze on grass already chewed flat to the ground. In the wide deep creek bed where only a trickle of water flowed in the summer, the skinny cows would wander, looking for new grass along winding paths splashed with manure.

Ayah pulled the old Army blanket over her head like a shawl. Jimmie's blanket—the one he had sent to her. That was a long time ago and the green wool was faded, and it was unraveling on the edges. She did not want to think about Jimmie. So she thought about the weaving and the way her mother had done it. On the tall wooden loom set into the sand under a tamarack tree for shade. She could see it clearly. She had been only a little girl when her grandma gave her the wooden combs to pull the twigs and burrs from the raw, freshly washed wool. And while she combed the wool, her grandma sat beside her, spinning a silvery strand of yarn around the smooth cedar spindle. Her mother worked at the loom with yarns dyed bright yellow and red and gold. She watched them dye the yarn in boiling black pots full of beeweed petals, juniper berries, and sage. The blankets her mother made were soft and woven so tight that rain rolled off them like birds' feathers. Ayah remembered sleeping warm on cold windy nights, wrapped in her mother's blankets on the hogan's sandy floor.

The snow drifted now, with the northwest wind hurling it in gusts. It drifted up around her black overshoes—old ones with little metal buckles. She smiled at the snow which was trying to cover her little by little. She could remember when they had no black rubber overshoes; only the high buckskin leggings that they wrapped over their elkhide moccasins. If the snow was dry or frozen, a person could walk all day and not get wet; and in the evenings the beams of the ceiling would hang with lengths of pale buckskin leggings, drying out slowly.

She felt peaceful remembering. She didn't feel cold any more. Jimmie's blanket seemed warmer than it had ever been. And she could remember the morning he was born. She could remember whispering to her mother, who was sleeping on the other side of the hogan, to tell her it was time now. She did not want to wake the others. The second time she called to her, her mother stood up and pulled on her shoes; she knew. They walked to the old stone hogan together, Ayah walking a step behind her mother. She waited alone, learning the rhythms of the pains while her mother went to call the old woman to help them. The morning was already warm even before dawn and Ayah smelled the bee flowers blooming and the young willow growing at the springs. She could remember that so clearly, but his birth merged into the births of the other children and to her it became all the same birth. They named him for the summer morning and in English they called him Jimmie.

It wasn't like Jimmie died. He just never came back, and one day a dark blue sedan with white writing on its doors pulled up in front of the box-car shack where the rancher let the Indians live. A man in a khaki uniform trimmed in gold gave them a yellow piece of paper and told them that Jimmie was dead. He said the Army would try to get the body back and then it would be shipped to them; but it wasn't likely because the helicopter had burned after it crashed. All of this was told to Chato because he could understand English. She stood inside the doorway holding the baby while Chato listened. Chato spoke English like a white man and he spoke Spanish too. He was taller than the white man and he stood straighter too. Chato didn't explain why; he just told the military man they could keep the body if they found it. The white man looked bewildered; he nodded his head and he left. Then Chato looked at her and shook his head, and then he told her, "Jimmie isn't coming home anymore," and when he spoke, he used the words to speak of the dead. She didn't cry then, but she hurt inside with anger. And she mourned him as the years passed, when a horse fell with Chato and broke his leg, and the white rancher told them he wouldn't pay Chato until he could work again. She mourned Jimmie because he would have worked for his father then; he would have saddled the big bay horse and ridden the fence lines each day, with wire cutters and heavy gloves, fixing the breaks in the barbed wire and putting the stray cattle back inside again.

She mourned him after the white doctors came to take Danny and Ella away. She was at the shack alone that day they came. It was back in the days before they hired Navajo women to go with them as interpreters. She recognized one of the doctors. She had seen him at the children's clinic at Cañoncito about a month ago. They were wearing khaki uniforms and they waved papers at her and a black ball-point pen, trying to make her understand their English words. She was frightened by the way they looked at the children, like the lizard watches the fly. Danny was swinging on the tire swing on the elm tree behind the rancher's house, and Ella was toddling around the front door, dragging the broomstick horse Chato made for her. Ayah could see they wanted her to sign the papers, and Chato had taught her to sign her name. It was something she was proud of. She only wanted them to go, and to take their eyes away from her children.

She took the pen from the man without looking at his face and she signed the papers in three different places he pointed to. She stared at the ground by their feet and waited for them to leave. But they stood there and began to point and gesture at the children. Danny stopped swinging. Ayah could see his fear. She moved suddenly and grabbed Ella into her arms; the child squirmed, trying to get back to her toys. Ayah ran with the baby toward Danny; she screamed for him to run and then she grabbed him around his chest and carried him too. She ran south into the foothills of juniper trees and black lava rock. Behind her she heard the doctors running, but they had been taken by surprise,

45

and as the hills became steeper and the cholla cactus were thicker, they stopped. When she reached the top of the hill, she stopped to listen in case they were circling around her. But in a few minutes she heard a car engine start and they drove away. The children had been too surprised to cry while she ran with them. Danny was shaking and Ella's little fingers were gripping Ayah's blouse.

She stayed up in the hills for the rest of the day, sitting on a black lava boulder in the sunshine where she could see for miles all around her. The sky was light blue and cloudless, and it was warm for late April. The sun warmth relaxed her and took the fear and anger away. She lay back on the rock and watched the sky. It seemed to her that she could walk into the sky, stepping through clouds endlessly. Danny played with little pebbles and stones, pretending they were birds eggs and then little rabbits. Ella sat at her feet and dropped fistfuls of dirt into the breeze, watching the dust and particles of sand intently. Ayah watched a hawk soar high above them, dark wings gliding; hunting or only watching, she did not know. The hawk was patient and he circled all afternoon before he disappeared around the high volcanic peak the Mexicans called Guadalupe.

Late in the afternoon, Ayah looked down at the gray boxcar shack with the paint all peeled from the wood; the stove pipe on the roof was rusted and crooked. The fire she had built that morning in the oil drum stove had burned out. Ella was asleep in her lap now and Danny sat close to her, complaining that he was hungry; he asked when they would go to the house. "We will stay up here until your father comes," she told him, "because those white men were chasing us." The boy remembered then and he nodded at her silently.

If Jimmie had been there he could have read those papers and explained to her what they said. Ayah would have known then, never to sign them. The doctors came back the next day and they brought a BIA policeman with them. They told Chato they had her signature and that was all they needed. Except for the kids. She listened to Chato sullenly; she hated him when he told her it was the old woman who died in the winter, spitting blood; it was her old grandma who had given the children this disease. "They don't spit blood," she said coldly. "The whites lie." She held Ella and Danny close to her, ready to run to the hills again. "I want a medicine man first," she said to Chato, not looking at him. He shook his head. "It's too late now. The policeman is with them. You signed the paper." His voice was gentle.

It was worse than if they had died: to lose the children and to know that somewhere, in a place called Colorado, in a place full of sick and dying strangers, her children were without her. There had been babies that died soon after they were born, and one that died before he could walk. She had carried them herself, up to the boulders and great pieces of the cliff that long ago crashed down from Long Mesa; she laid them in the crevices of sandstone and buried them in fine brown sand with round quartz pebbles that washed down the hills in the rain. She had endured it because they had been with her. But she could not bear this pain. She did not sleep for a long time after they took her children. She stayed on the hill where they had fled the first time, and she slept rolled up in the blanket Jimmie had sent her. She carried the pain in her belly and it was fed by everything she saw: the blue sky of their last day together and the dust and pebbles they played with; the swing in the elm tree and broomstick horse choked life from her. The pain filled her stomach and there was no room for food or for her lungs to fill with air. The air and the food would have been theirs.

She hated Chato, not because he let the police-man and doctors put the screaming children in the government car, but because he had taught her to sign her name. Because it was like the old ones always told her about learning their language or any of their ways: it endangered you. She slept alone on the hill until the middle of November when the first snows came. Then she made a bed for herself where the children had slept. She did not lie down beside Chato again until many years later, when he was sick and shivering and only her body could keep him warm. The illness came after the white rancher told Chato he was too old to work for him any-more, and Chato and his old woman should be out of the shack by the next afternoon because the rancher had hired new people to work there. That had satisfied her. To see how the white man repaid Chato's years of loyalty and work. All of Chato's fine-sounding English talk didn't change things.

It snowed steadily and the luminous light from the snow gradually diminished into the darkness. Somewhere in Cebolleta a dog barked and other village dogs joined with it. Ayah looked in the direction she had come, from the bar where Chato was buying the wine. Sometimes he told her to go on ahead and wait; and then he never came. And when she finally went back looking for him, she would find him passed out at the bottom of the wooden steps to Azzie's Bar. All the wine would be gone and most of the money too, from the pale blue check that came to them once a month in a government envelope. It was then that she would look at his face and his hands, scarred by ropes and the barbed wire of all those years, and she would think, this man is a stranger; for forty years she had smiled at him and cooked his food, but he remained a stranger. She stood up again, with the snow almost to her knees, and she walked back to find Chato.

It was hard to walk in the deep snow and she felt the air burn in her lungs. She stopped a short distance from the bar to rest and readjust the blanket. But this time he wasn't waiting for her on the bottom step with his old Stetson hat pulled down and his shoulders hunched up in his long wool overcoat.

She was careful not to slip on the wooden steps. When she pushed the door open, warm air and cigarette smoke hit her face. She looked around slowly and deliberately, in every corner, in every dark place that the old man might find

to sleep. The bar owner didn't like Indians in there, especially Navajos, but he let Chato come in because he could talk Spanish like he was one of them. The men at the bar stared at her, and the bartender saw that she left the door open wide. Snowflakes were flying inside like moths and melting into a puddle on the oiled wood floor. He motioned to her to close the door, but she did not see him. She held herself straight and walked across the room slowly, searching the room with every step. The snow in her hair melted and she could feel it on her forehead. At the far corner of the room, she saw red flames at the mica window of the old stove door; she looked behind the stove just to make sure. The bar got quiet except for the Spanish polka music playing on the jukebox. She stood by the stove and shook the snow from her blanket and held it near the stove to dry. The wet wool smell reminded her of new-born goats in early March, brought inside to warm near the fire. She felt calm.

In past years they would have told her to get out. But her hair was white now and her face was wrinkled. They looked at her like she was a spider crawling slowly across the room. They were afraid; she could feel the fear. She looked at their faces steadily. They reminded her of the first time the white people brought her children back to her that winter. Danny had been shy and hid behind the thin white woman who brought them. And the baby had not known her until Ayah took her into her arms, and then Ella had nuzzled close to her as she had when she was nursing. The blonde woman was nervous and kept looking at a dainty gold watch on her wrist. She sat on the bench near the small window and watched the dark snow clouds gather around the mountains; she was worrying about the unpaved road. She was frightened by what she saw inside too: the strips of venison drying on a rope across the ceiling and the children jabbering excitedly in a language she did not know. So they stayed for only a few hours. Ayah watched the government car disappear down the road and she knew they were already being weaned from these lava hills and from this sky. The last time they came was in early June, and Ella stared at her the way the men in the bar were now staring. Ayah did not try to pick her up; she smiled at her instead and spoke cheerfully to Danny. When he tried to answer her, he could not seem to remember and he spoke English words with the Navajo. But he gave her a scrap of paper that he had found somewhere and carried in his pocket; it was folded in half, and he shyly looked up at her and said it was a bird. She asked Chato if they were home for good this time. He spoke to the white woman and she shook her head. "How much longer?" he asked, and she said she didn't know; but Chato saw how she stared at the boxcar shack. Ayah turned away then. She did not say good-bye.

She felt satisfied that the men in the bar feared her. Maybe it was her face and the way she held her mouth with teeth clenched tight, like there was nothing anyone could do to her now. She walked north down the road, searching for the old man. She did this because she had the blanket, and there would be no place for him except with her and the blanket in the old adobe barn near the arroyo. They always slept there when they came to Cebolleta. If the money and the wine were gone, she would be relieved because then they could go home again; back to the old hogan with a dirt roof and rock walls where she herself had been born. And the next day the old man could go back to the few sheep they still had, to follow along behind them, guiding them, into dry sandy arroyos where sparse grass grew.

49

She knew he did not like walking behind old ewes when for so many years he rode big quarter horses and worked with cattle. But she wasn't sorry for him; he should have known all along what would happen.

There had not been enough rain for their garden in five years; and that was when Chato finally hitched a ride into the town and brought back brown boxes of rice and sugar and big tin cans of welfare peaches. After that, at the first of the month they went to Cebolleta to ask the postmaster for the check; and then Chato would go to the bar and cash it. They did this as they planted the garden every May, not because anything would survive the summer dust, but because it was time to do this. The journey passed the days that smelled silent and dry like the caves above the canyon with yellow painted buffaloes on their walls.

He was walking along the pavement when she found him. He did not stop or turn around when he heard her behind him. She walked beside him and she noticed how slowly he moved now. He smelled strong of woodsmoke and urine. Lately he had been forgetting. Sometimes he called her by his sister's name and she had been gone for a long time. Once she had found him wandering on the road to the white man's ranch, and she asked him why he was going that way; he laughed at her and said, "You know they can't run that ranch without me," and he walked on determined, limping on the leg that had been crushed many years before. Now he looked at her curiously, as if for the first time, but he kept shuffling along, moving slowly along the side of the highway. His gray hair had grown long and spread out on the shoulders of the long overcoat. He wore the old felt hat pulled down over his ears. His boots were worn out at the toes and he had stuffed pieces of an old red shirt in the holes. The rags made his feet look like little animals up to their ears in snow. She laughed at his feet; the snow muffled the sound of her laugh. He stopped and looked at her again. The wind had quit blowing and the snow was falling straight down; the southeast sky was beginning to clear and Ayah could see a star.

"Let's rest awhile," she said to him. They walked away from the road and up the slope to the giant boulders that had tumbled down from the red sandrock mesa throughout the centuries of rainstorms and earth tremors. In a place where the boulders shut out the wind, they sat down with their backs against the rock. She offered half of the blanket to him and they sat wrapped together.

The storm passed swiftly. The clouds moved east. They were massive and full, crowding together across the sky. She watched them with the feeling of horses—steely blue-gray horses startled across the sky. The powerful haunches pushed into the distances and the tail hairs streamed white mist behind them. The sky cleared. Ayah saw that there was nothing between her and the stars. The light was crystalline. There was no shimmer, no distortion through earth haze. She breathed the clarity of the night sky; she smelled the purity of the half moon and the stars. He was lying on his side with his knees pulled up near his belly for warmth. His eyes were closed now, and in the light from the stars and the moon, he looked young again.

She could see it descend out of the night sky: an icy stillness from the edge of the thin moon. She recognized the freezing. It came gradually, sinking snowflake by snowflake until the crust was heavy and deep. It had the strength of the stars in Orion, and its journey was endless. Ayah knew that with the wine he would sleep. He would not feel it. She tucked the blanket around

him, remembering how it was when Ella had been with her; and she felt the rush so big inside her heart for the babies. And she sang the only song she knew to sing for babies. She could not remember if she had ever sung it to her children, but she knew that her grandmother had sung it and her mother had sung it:

The earth is your mother,
*   she holds you.*
The sky is your father,
*   he protects you.*
Sleep,
sleep.
Rainbow is your sister,
*   she loves you.*
The winds are your brothers,
*   they sing to you.*
Sleep,
sleep.
We are together always
We are together always
There never was a time
when this
was not so.

Grandma Lillie was born in Los Lunas, New Mexico. She was baptized "Francesca," but her father, my great-grandpa Stagner, called her "Lillie" after one of his sisters he left behind in Texas when he ran away from home with his brother, Bill. Nobody knows for sure why great-grandpa and his brother ran away when they weren't more than fourteen and fifteen or why it was twenty years before great-grandpa ever let them know where he was. Maybe it had something to do with the times, and the place his father had settled, near Sweetwater, Texas. My great-grandfather's father had married an Indian woman, Rhoda Touchstone, and then had left Indian country. I have been told by Mrs. Virginia Pearl that at about that time, white settlers coming to the Oklahoma land rush began to threaten Indian families, especially families where intermarriage had taken place. Mrs. Pearl's family was such a family, and she remembers that at fourteen she drove a wagon from southern Oklahoma all the way to Casas Grandes, Mexico, as a group of her people went searching for a place they might live without harassment. They were called the Wagon People because they had no place anymore once the bigotry arrived in Oklahoma. The only reason Arizona and New Mexico offered a home for them was because the white people here were so worried about Apaches they didn't notice these Cherokee half-breeds.

What Whirlwind Man Told Kochininako, Yellow Woman
    I myself belong to the wind
    and so it is we will travel swiftly
    this whole world
    with dust and with windstorms.

YELLOW WOMAN

My thigh clung to his with dampness, and I watched the sun rising up through the tamaracks and willows. The small brown water birds came to the river and hopped across the mud, leaving brown scratches in the alkali-white crust. They bathed in the river silently. I could hear the water, almost at our feet where the narrow fast channel bubbled and washed green ragged moss and fern leaves. I looked at him beside me, rolled in the red blanket on the white river sand. I cleaned the sand out of the cracks between my toes, squinting because the sun was above the willow trees. I looked at him for the last time, sleeping on the white river sand.

I felt hungry and followed the river south the way we had come the afternoon before, following our footprints that were already blurred by lizard tracks and bug trails. The horses were still lying down, and the black one whinnied when he saw me but he did not get up—maybe it was because the corral was made out of thick cedar branches and the horses had not yet felt the sun like I had. I tried to look beyond the pale red mesas to the pueblo. I knew it was there, even if I could not see it, on the sandrock hill above the river, the same river that moved past me now and had reflected the moon last night.

The horse felt warm underneath me. He shook his head and pawed the sand. The bay whinnied and leaned against the gate trying to follow, and I remembered him asleep in the red blanket beside the river. I slid off the horse and tied him close to the other horse, I walked north with the river again, and the white sand broke loose in footprints over footprints.

"Wake up."

He moved in the blanket and turned his face to me with his eyes still closed. I knelt down to touch him.

"I'm leaving."

He smiled now, eyes still closed. "You are coming with me, remember?" He sat up now with his bare dark chest and belly in the sun.

"Where?"

"To my place."

"And will I come back?"

He pulled his pants on. I walked away from him, feeling him behind me and smelling the willows.

"Yellow Woman," he said.

I turned to face him. "Who are you?" I asked.

He laughed and knelt on the low, sandy bank, washing his face in the river. "Last night you guessed my name, and you knew why I had come."

I stared past him at the shallow moving water and tried to remember the night, but I could only see the moon in the water and remember his warmth around me.

"But I only said that you were him and that I was Yellow Woman—I'm not really her—I have my own name and I come from the pueblo on the other side of the mesa. Your name is Silva and you are a stranger I met by the river yesterday afternoon."

He laughed softly. "What happened yesterday has nothing to do with what you will do today, Yellow Woman."

"I know—that's what I'm saying—the old stories about the ka'tsina spirit and Yellow Woman can't mean us."

My old grandpa liked to tell those stories best. There is one about Badger and Coyote who went hunting and were gone all day, and when the sun was going down they found a house. There was a girl living there alone, and she had light hair and eyes and she told them that they could sleep with her. Coyote wanted to be with her all night so he sent Badger into a prairie-dog hole, telling him he thought he saw something in it. As soon as Badger crawled in, Coyote blocked up the entrance with rocks and hurried back to Yellow Woman.

"Come here," he said gently.

He touched my neck and I moved close to him to feel his breathing and to hear his heart. I was wondering if Yellow Woman had known who she was—if she knew that she would become part of the stories. Maybe she'd had another name that her husband and relatives called her so that only the ka'tsina from the north and the storytellers would know her as Yellow Woman. But I didn't go on; I felt him all around me, pushing me down into the white river sand.

Yellow Woman went away with the spirit from the north and lived with him and his relatives. She was gone for a long time, but then one day she came back and she brought twin boys.

"Do you know the story?"

"What story?" He smiled and pulled me close to him as he said this. I was afraid lying there on the red blanket. All I could know was the way he felt, warm, damp, his body beside me. This is the way it happens in the stories, I was thinking, with no thought beyond the moment she meets the ka'tsina spirit and they go.

"I don't have to go. What they tell in stories was real only then, back in time immemorial, like they say."

He stood up and pointed at my clothes tangled in the blanket. "Let's go," he said.

I walked beside him, breathing hard because he walked fast, his hand around my wrist. I had stopped trying to pull away from him, because his hand felt cool and the sun was high, drying the river bed into alkali. I will see someone, eventually I will see someone, and then I will be certain that he is only a man—some man from nearby—and I will be sure that I am not Yellow Woman. Because she is from out of time past and

I live now and I've been to school and there are highways and pickup trucks that Yellow Woman never saw.

It was an easy ride north on horseback. I watched the change from the cottonwood trees along the river to the junipers that brushed past us in the foothills, and finally there were only piñons, and when I looked up at the rim of the mountain plateau I could see pine trees growing on the edge. Once I stopped to look down, but the pale sandstone had disappeared and the river was gone and the dark lava hills were all around. He touched my hand, not speaking, but always singing softly a mountain song and looking into my eyes.

I felt hungry and wondered what they were doing at home now—my mother, my grandmother, my husband, and the baby. Cooking breakfast, saying, "Where did she go?—maybe kidnapped." And Al going to the tribal police with the details: "She went walking along the river."

The house was made with black lava rock and red mud. It was high above the spreading miles of arroyos and long mesas. I smelled a mountain smell of pitch and buck brush. I stood there beside the black horse, looking down on the small, dim country we had passed, and I shivered.

"Yellow Woman, come inside where it's warm."

56

He lit a fire in the stove. It was an old stove with a round belly and an enamel coffeepot on top. There was only the stove, some faded Navajo blankets, and a bedroll and cardboard box. The floor was made of smooth adobe plaster, and there was one small window facing east. He pointed at the box.

"There's some potatoes and the frying pan." He sat on the floor with his arms around his knees pulling them close to his chest and he watched me fry the potatoes. I didn't mind him watching me because he was always watching me—he had been watching me since I came upon him sitting on the river bank trimming leaves from a willow twig with his knife. We ate from the pan and he wiped the grease from his fingers on his Levi's.

"Have you brought women here before?" He smiled and kept chewing, so I said, "Do you always use the same tricks?"

"What tricks?" He looked at me like he didn't understand.

"The story about being a ka'tsina from the mountains. The story about Yellow Woman."

Silva was silent; his face was calm.

"I don't believe it. Those stories couldn't happen now," I said.

He shook his head and said softly, "But someday they will talk about us, and they will say, 'Those two lived long ago when things like that happened.'"

He stood up and went out. I ate the rest of the potatoes and thought about things—about the noise the stove was making and the sound of the mountain wind outside. I remembered yesterday and the day before, and then I went outside.

I walked past the corral to the edge where the narrow trail cut through the black rim rock. I was standing in the sky with nothing around me but the wind that came down from the blue mountain peak behind me. I could see faint mountain images in the distance miles across the vast spread of mesas and valleys and plains. I wondered who was over there to feel the mountain wind on those sheer blue edges—who walks on the pine needles in those blue mountains.

"Can you see the pueblo?" Silva was standing behind me.

I shook my head. "We're too far away."

"From here I can see the world." He stepped out on the edge. "The Navajo reservation begins over there." He pointed to the east. "The Pueblo boundaries are over here." He looked below us to

57

the south, where the narrow trail seemed to come from. "The Texans have their ranches over there, starting with that valley, the Concho Valley. The Mexicans run some cattle over there too."

"Do you ever work for them?"

"I steal from them," Silva answered. The sun was dropping behind us and the shadows were filling the land below. I turned away from the edge that dropped forever into the valleys below.

"I'm cold," I said, "I'm going inside." I started wondering about this man who could speak the Pueblo language so well but who lived on a mountain and rustled cattle. I decided that this man Silva must be Navajo, because Pueblo men didn't do things like that.

"You must be a Navajo."

Silva shook his head gently. "Little Yellow Woman," he said, "you never give up, do you? I have told you who I am. The Navajo people know me, too." He knelt down and unrolled the bedroll and spread the extra blankets out on a piece of canvas. The sun was down, and the only light in the house came from outside—the dim orange light from sundown.

I stood there and waited for him to crawl under the blankets.

"What are you waiting for?" he said, and I lay down beside him. He undressed me slowly like the night before beside the river—kissing my face gently and running his hands up and down my belly and legs. He took off my pants and then he laughed.

"Why are you laughing?"

"You are breathing so hard."

I pulled away from him and turned my back to him.

He pulled me around and pinned me down with his arms and chest. "You don't understand, do you, little Yellow Woman? You will do what I want."

And again he was all around me with his skin slippery against mine, and I was afraid because I understood that his strength could hurt me. I lay underneath him and I knew that he could destroy me. But later, while he slept beside me, I touched his face and I had a feeling—the kind of feeling for him that overcame me that morning along the river. I kissed him on the forehead and he reached out for me.

When I woke up in the morning he was gone. It gave me a strange feeling because for a long time I sat there on the blankets and looked around the little house for some object of his—some proof that he had been there or maybe that he was coming back. Only the blankets and the cardboard box remained. The .30-30 that had been leaning in the corner was gone, and so was the knife I had used the night before. He was gone, and I had my chance to go now. But first I had to eat, because I knew it would be a long walk home.

I found some dried apricots in the cardboard box, and I sat down on a rock at the edge of the plateau rim. There was no wind and the sun warmed me. I was surrounded by silence. I drowsed with apricots in my mouth, and I didn't believe that there were highways or railroads or cattle to steal.

When I woke up, I stared down at my feet in the black mountain dirt. Little black ants were swarming over the pine needles around my foot. They must have smelled the apricots. I thought about my family far below me. They would be wondering about me, because this had never happened to me before. The tribal police would file a report. But if old Grandpa weren't dead he would tell them what happened—he would laugh and say, "Stolen by a ka'tsina, a mountain spirit. She'll come home—they usually do." There are enough of them to handle things. My mother and grandmother will raise the baby like they raised me. Al will find someone else, and they will go on like before, except that there will be a story about the day I disappeared while I was walking along the river. Silva had come for me; he said he had. I did not decide to go. I just went. Moon-flowers blossom in the sand hills before dawn, just as I followed him. That's what I was thinking as I wandered along the trail through the pine trees.

It was noon when I got back. When I saw the stone house I remembered that I had meant to go home. But that didn't seem important any more, maybe because there were little blue flowers growing in the meadow behind the stone house and the gray squirrels were playing in the pines next to the house. The horses were standing in the corral, and there was a beef carcass hanging on the shady side of a big pine in front of the house. Flies buzzed around the clotted blood that hung from the carcass. Silva was washing his hands in a bucket full of water. He must have heard me coming because he spoke to me without turning to face me.

"I've been waiting for you."

"I went walking in the big pine trees."

I looked into the bucket full of bloody water with brown-and-white animal hairs floating in it. Silva stood there letting his hand drip, examining me intently.

"Are you coming with me?"

"Where?" I asked him.

"To sell the meat in Marquez."

"If you're sure it's O.K."

"I wouldn't ask you if it wasn't," he answered.

He sloshed the water around in the bucket before he dumped it out and set the bucket upside down near the door. I followed him to the corral and watched him saddle the horses. Even beside the horses he looked tall, and I asked him again if he wasn't Navajo. He didn't say anything; he just shook his head and kept cinching up the saddle.

"But Navajos are tall."

"Get on the horse," he said, "and let's go."

The last thing he did before we started down the steep trail was to grab the .30-30 from the corner. He slid the rifle into the scabbard that hung from his saddle.

"Do they ever try to catch you?" I asked.

"They don't know who I am."

"Then why did you bring the rifle?"

"Because we are going to Marquez where the Mexicans live."

The trail leveled out on a narrow ridge that was steep on both sides like an animal spine. On one side I could see where the trail went around the rocky gray hills and disappeared into the south-east where the pale sandrock mesas stood in the distance near my home. On the other side was a trail that went west, and as I looked far into the distance I thought I saw the little town. But Silva said no, that I was looking in the wrong place, that I just thought I saw houses. After that I quit looking off into the distance; it was hot and the wildflowers were closing up their deep-yellow petals. Only the waxy cactus flowers bloomed in the bright sun, and I saw every color that a cactus blossom can be; the white ones and the red ones were still buds, but the purple and the yellow were blossoms, open full and the most beautiful of all.

Silva saw him before I did. The white man was riding a big gray horse, coming up the trail towards us. He was traveling fast and the gray horse's feet sent rocks rolling off the trail into the dry tumbleweeds. Silva motioned for me to stop and we watched the white man. He didn't see us right away, but finally his horse whinnied at our horses and he stopped. He looked at us briefly before he lapped the gray horse across the three hundred yards that separated us. He stopped his horse in front of Silva, and his young fat face was shadowed by the brim of his hat. He didn't look mad, but his small, pale eyes moved from the blood-soaked gunny sacks hanging from my saddle to Silva's face and then back to my face.

"Where did you get the fresh meat?" the white man asked.

"I've been hunting," Silva said, and when he shifted his weight in the saddle the leather creaked.

"The hell you have, Indian. You've been rustling cattle. We've been looking for the thief for a long time."

The rancher was fat, and sweat began to soak through his white cowboy shirt and the wet cloth stuck to the thick rolls of belly fat. He almost seemed to be panting from the exertion of talking, and he smelled rancid, maybe because Silva scared him.

Silva turned to me and smiled. "Go back up the mountain, Yellow Woman."

The white man got angry when he heard Silva speak in a language he couldn't understand. "Don't try anything, Indian. Just keep riding to Marquez. We'll call the state police from there."

The rancher must have been unarmed because he was very frightened and if he had a gun he would have pulled it out then. I turned my horse around and the rancher yelled, "Stop!" I looked at Silva for an instant and there was something ancient and dark—something I could feel in my stomach—in his eyes, and when I glanced at his hand I saw his finger on the trigger of the .30–30 that was still in the saddle scabbard. I slapped my horse across the flank and the sacks of raw meat swung against my knees as the horse leaped up the trail. It was hard to keep my balance, and once I thought I felt the saddle slipping backward; it was because of this that I could not look back.

I didn't stop until I reached the ridge where the trail forked. The horse was breathing deep gasps and there was a dark film of sweat on its neck. I looked down in the direction I had come from, but I couldn't see the place. I waited. The wind came up and pushed warm air past me. I looked up at the sky, pale blue and full of thin clouds and fading vapor trails left by jets.

I think four shots were fired—I remember hearing four hollow explosions that reminded me of deer hunting. There could have been more shots after that, but I couldn't have heard them because my horse was running again and the loose rocks were making too much noise as they scattered around his feet.

Horses have a hard time running downhill, but I went that way instead of uphill to the mountain because I thought it was safer. I felt better with the horse running southeast past the round gray hills that were covered with cedar trees and black lava rock. When I got to the plain in the distance I could see the dark green patches of tamaracks that grew along the river; and beyond the river I could see the beginning of the pale sandrock mesas. I stopped the horse and looked back to see if anyone was coming; then I got off the horse and turned the horse around, wondering if it would go back to its corral under the pines on the mountain. It looked back at me for a moment and then plucked a mouthful of green tumbleweeds before it trotted back up the trail with its ears pointed forward, carrying its head daintily to one side to avoid stepping on the dragging reins. When the horse disappeared over the last hill, the gunny sacks full of meat were still swinging and bouncing.

I walked toward the river on a wood-hauler's road that I knew would eventually lead to the paved road. I was thinking about waiting beside the road for someone to drive by, but by the time I got to the pavement I had decided it wasn't very far to walk if I followed the river back the way Silva and I had come.

The river water tasted good, and I sat in the shade under a cluster of silvery willows. I thought about Silva, and I felt sad at leaving him; still, there was something strange about him, and I tried to figure it out all the way back home.

I came back to the place on the river bank where he had been sitting the first time I saw him. The green willow leaves that he had trimmed from the branch were still lying there, wilted in the sand. I saw the leaves and I wanted to go back to him—to kiss him and to touch him— but the mountains were too far away now. And I told myself, because I believe it, he will come back sometime and be waiting again by the river.

I followed the path up from the river into the village. The sun was getting low, and I could smell supper cooking when I got to the screen door of my house. I could hear their voices inside—my mother was telling my grandmother how to fix the Jell-O and my husband, Al, was playing with the baby. I decided to tell them that some Navajo had kidnaped me, but I was sorry that old Grandpa wasn't alive to hear my story because it was the Yellow Woman stories he liked to tell best.

COTTONWOOD *Part One: Story of Sun House*

Cottonwood,
        cottonwood.
                It was under the cottonwood tree
                in a sandy wash of the big canyon
                        under the tree you can find
                    even now
                                among all the others
                                this tree
                        where she came to wait for him.
                                                "You will know,"
                                                he said
                                                "you will know by the colors—

                                                cottonwood leaves
                                                more colors of the sun
                                                than the sun himself."
                                    (But you see, he *was* the Sun,
                                      he was only pretending to be
                                      a human being.)

When the light
from the autumn edge of the sky
touched only the north canyon walls
                (south walls in shadow)
When day balanced once more with night

it was the season
to go again
to find the place.

She left precise stone rooms
that hold the heart silently
She walked past white corn
hung in long rows from roof beams
the dry husks rattled in a thin autumn wind.

She left her home
her clan
and the people
(three small children
the youngest just weaned
her husband away cutting firewood)

She left for the place located
only by the colors of the sun.

"Travel across the swirled sandstone
go until you find a tree
distinct from all the others,"
he told her
"Only in this way
though it has not happened before.
You must
though the people may not understand."

(All this was happening long time ago, see?)
Before that time, there were no stories

about drastic things which
must be done
      for the world
      to continue

Out of love for this earth

          cottonwood
          sandstone
          and sky.

    She had been with him
only once.
      His eyes (the light in them had blinded her)
so she had never seen him
only his eyes
      and she did not know how to find him
      except by the cottonwood tree.

          "In a canyon of cloudy sky stone,"
             he told her (he was describing the Sun House then
               but she did not know that)

        "Colors—
          more colors than the sun has
        You will know that way,
           you will know."

"But what if
                    the colors have faded
                    the leaves fallen already and scattered
                    the tree lost among all the others
                                their pale branches bare
            How then will I find you?"

She had to outrun the long night
                    its freezing
                    approaching steadily

She had to find the place
                    before the winter constellations
                    closed around the sky forever
                    before the last chill silenced the earth.

            "Kochininako, Yellow Woman, welcome,"
                    and he came out from the southeast to greet her.
                    He came out of the Sun House again.

And so the earth continued
as it has since that time.

Cottonwood,
          cottonwood.

So much depends
          upon one in the great canyon.

COTTONWOOD *Part Two: Buffalo Story*

In those days
sometimes the people didn't have very much meat.
When it got dry
the deer went too high on the mountains
and the people only had a little rabbit meat
if they were lucky.

When it got so dry
nothing was growing
none of the plants
and there was no corn
or beans
they would be hungry then
the children would cry
but still there was nothing to eat
no food.

It was one of those times
one of those times when
there had been no rain for months
and everything was drying up.

It was at this time
long ago
Kochininako, Yellow Woman went searching
for water to carry back to her family.
She went first to the spring
near the village
but the water had dried up
the earth there
wasn't even damp when she touched it.

So she had to walk farther
much farther toward the east
looking for water.
And finally
when she had gone a long distance to the east
she found a pool at a sharp curve
in an arroyo.
But when she got to that pool
the water was churning and muddy.

She was afraid
because she knew something had just been there
something very large had muddied the water.

And just as she turned to hurry away
because she didn't want to find out
what giant animal had been there
she saw him.
She saw him tying his leggings
drops of water were still shining on his chest.
He was very good to look at
and she kept looking at him
because she had never seen anyone like him.
It was Buffalo Man who was very beautiful.
          "Come with me,"
                              he said, and he smiled at her.
          "No, I must carry this water back home.
          My family needs this water," she said
                              but she was still looking
                              at him.
          "You shouldn't have gone so far away
            from your village,"
                              he said
          "Because now you are here
            and this is where we are—
            the Buffalo People."
So he grabbed her
and he put her on his back
and carried her away.
They went very fast
and she couldn't escape him.

Back at home
they started to worry
because she always came back right away
and they wondered what happened.
Her husband Estoy-eh-muut, Arrowboy
waited all night for her
he sat on the east edge of the village
and watched for her
but she did not come.
Right before dawn
the Big Star
the Morning Star came and said to him,

              "Ahmoo'uut, you are looking for Kochininako.
              Well, I saw her this morning
              as I came up from the East.
              Buffalo Man has taken her over there."
So Estoy-eh-muut went to find Spider Woman
because she knew many things
and maybe she could help him.

She was sitting in her place
at the base of a bee weed plant.
When she saw him she said,

              "Ahmoo'uut, grandson, how are things?"
And Estoy-eh-muut said,
             "Oh Grandmother
              the Big Star told me

                    Buffalo Man has taken Kochininako.
                    He has taken her away to the East country."
"My, my," old Spider Woman said
"Now Grandson, don't worry.
I have something that will help you."
Then she gave him
a buckskin pouch
full of red clay dust.
                    "Those Buffalo People
                    will not easily give her up.
                    They'll chase after you
                    and try to trample you.
                    And when they do
                    you take this dust
                    and throw it in their eyes."
So he gave her sweet corn pollen
and he thanked her for her help
and he started traveling East.
He went a long distance
and finally he came to the wide plains
where the buffalo grass was growing
as high as his chest.

Off in the distance
he could see the Buffalo People
and there were four big bull buffalo
standing guard.

Estoy-eh-muut crawled very carefully
through the tall grass
and when he got close enough
he threw the red clay dust
and he blinded each one of the buffalo guards.

As fast as he could
he found Kochininako.
She was sleeping in the tall grass
some distance from the buffalo.
                              "Hurry!" he told her,
                                Run as fast as you can!"
She seemed to
get up a little slowly
but he didn't think much of it then.

He took her hand
and they started running
because by this time
the Buffalo People knew what had happened
and they were looking for them,
in a big herd the Buffalo People
were chasing after them.

Buffalo Man sent hail storms
in big clouds
trying to slow them down
72   but Estoy-eh-muut blew the red clay dust

at the hail storm clouds
and stopped them.

Finally Estoy-eh-muut noticed
that Kochininako was running slower and slower
so they stopped to rest
at a cottonwood tree
growing by itself
on the plains.
About that time
Estoy-eh-muut saw a big cloud of dust
raised by the buffalo feet
and he knew they were coming
so he and Kochininako climbed the cottonwood tree.

Very soon the buffalo came
one after another
they galloped
right under the cottonwood tree.
The very last one
was a young buffalo calf
who was tiring from the long chase.
He stopped under the cottonwood tree
to rest.

Her urine sprinkled down on his back
and the buffalo calf looked up
and he called to the others

"Come back! Come back!
Our sister-in-law is here
sitting up in this tree."

The buffaloes turned and came running back.
They stood around the tree in a big circle
and Buffalo Man lowered his head
and went running at the cottonwood tree.
He was going to butt down the tree
and get Estoy-eh-muut and Kochininako.
But just as Buffalo Man was running at the tree
Estoy-eh-muut shot him with an arrow
and Buffalo Man fell dead.
Then Estoy-eh-muut killed all the others—
all those buffalo standing around the tree
he shot them with his bow and arrows.
                    "Go home," he told Kochininako.
                    "Go home and tell the people to come.
                     Now we have plenty of meat
                     and no one will be hungry anymore.
                     Go tell them to come."
But Kochininako
wouldn't come down
out of that cottonwood tree
He saw she had tears in her eyes.
                         "What's wrong?
                          Why are you crying," he asked her.

"Because you killed them,"
                                    she said.
"I suppose you love them,"
                        Estoy-eh-muut said,
"and you want to stay with them."
And Kochininako nodded her head
and then he killed her too
and he carried her body to her sisters
and they went with him to their father.

When their father saw that Kochininako was dead
he started crying and shaking his head
and calling her name
Estoy-eh-muut told him
                "I killed her
                 because she wanted to stay with the Buffalo People
                 she wanted to go with them
                 and now she is with them."
The old man, her father, cried
                "A'moo-ooh Kochininako
                 A'moo-ooh, my daughter.
                 You have gone away with them!"
Then they all left the village
all the people went toward the East
and they found the cottonwood tree
where all the dead buffalo were lying.
They cut up the meat and dried it—

they made buffalo jerky
and they carried it home.
This meat lasted them a long time.
So that was the beginning—
the hunters would travel
far away to plains in the East
where the Buffalo People lived
and they would bring home
all that good meat.
Nobody would be hungry then.

It was all because
one time long ago
our daughter, our sister Kochininako
went away with them.

THE TIME WE CLIMBED SNAKE MOUNTAIN

Seeing good places
    for my hands
I grab the warm parts of the cliff
            and I feel the mountain as I climb.

Somewhere around here
        yellow spotted snake is sleeping on his rock
                in the sun.

So
    please, I tell them
            watch out,
don't step on the spotted yellow snake
                    he lives here.
The mountain is his.

＊＊

When I was thirteen I carried an old .30–30 we borrowed from George Pearl. It was an old Winchester that had a steel ring on its side to secure it in a saddle scabbard. It was heavy and hurt my shoulder when I fired it and it seemed even louder than my father's larger caliber rifle, but I didn't say anything because I was so happy to be hunting for the first time. I didn't get a deer that year but one afternoon hunting alone on the round volcanic hill we called Chato, I saw a giant brown bear lying in the sun below the hilltop. Dead or just sleeping, I couldn't tell. I was cautious because I already knew what hours of searching for motion, for the outline of a deer, for the color of a deer's hide can do to the imagination. I already knew how easily the weathered branches of a dead juniper could resemble antlers because I had walked with my father on hunts since I was eight. So I stood motionless for a long time until my breathing was more calm and my heart wasn't beating so hard. I even shifted my eyes away for a moment hoping to see my uncle

Polly or my cousin Richard who was hunting the ridges nearby.

I knew there were no bears that large on Mt. Taylor; I was pretty sure there were no bears that large anywhere. But when I looked back at the slope above me, the giant brown bear was still lying on the sunny slope of the hill above patches of melting snow and tall yellow grass. I watched it for a long time, for any sign of motion, for its breathing, but I wasn't close enough to tell for sure. If it was dead I wanted to be able to examine it up close. It occurred to me that I could fire my rifle over its head but I knew better than to wake a bear with only a .30–30. All this time I had only moved my eyes, and my arms were getting numb from holding the rifle in the same position for so long. As quietly and as care-fully as I probably will ever move, I turned and walked away from the giant bear, still down wind from it. After I had gone a distance down the slope I stopped to look back to see if it was still a giant brown bear sunning itself on one of the last warm afternoons of the year, and not just damp brown earth and a lightning-struck log above the snow patches. But the big dark bear remained there, on the south slope of Chato, with its head facing southeast, the eyes closed, motionless. I hurried the rest of the way down the ridge, listen-ing closely to the wind at my back for sounds, glancing over my shoulder now and then.

I never told anyone what I had seen because I knew they don't let people who see such things carry .30-30's or hunt deer with them.

Two years later, on the north side of Chato, my Uncle
Polly was rewarded for his patience by the "old man
of the mountain" as my uncle had called him—the mule
deer whose antlers were as wide as a gun rack. As soon
as the big buck had gone down, Uncle Polly signaled
so those of us close by could go help.
As I cut across the south slope to reach my Uncle
I realized it was middle afternoon almost the same
time of day as before, except this year no snow
had fallen yet.
I walked past the place deliberately.
I found no bones, but when a wind moved through the
light yellow grass that afternoon I hurried around the
hill to find my uncle.
Sleeping, not dead, I decided.

Aunt Alice told my sisters and me this story one
time when she came to stay with us while our
parents had gone up to Mt. Taylor deer hunting.
I was seven years old the last time I had to stay
behind. And I felt very sad about not getting to
go hunting. Maybe that's why Aunt Alice told us
this story.

Once there was a young Laguna girl
who was a fine hunter
who hunted deer and rabbits
just like the boys and the men did.
You know there have been laguna women
who were good hunters
who could hunt as well as any of the men.
The girl's name was Kochininako and
she would go out hunting
and bring home rabbits
sometimes deer
whatever she could find
she'd bring them home to her mother and her sisters.
This one time
she had been hunting
all morning
south of Laguna village

a distance past the sand hills
and she thought
she would start toward home.
She was just coming past
Tchi mu yah a mesa
when she met up with
a great big animal
called *Estrucuyu.*
Estrucuyu was some kind of giant
they had back in those days
The giant *Estrucuyu* saw the rabbits
Kochininako had hanging from her belt
she had four or five big rabbits
she had gotten that morning.
And he asked her
if she would throw him one of the rabbits.
So she did
and he just gobbled it up
in a minute's time
because he was so big.
He had a great big head
and he asked for another one
and another one.
Pretty soon
she threw
every one of the rabbits
she had
to this *Estrucuyu*

and he just swallowed them
like they were little crumbs.
Then the giant   said,
    "What else do you have
     to give me?"
And Kochininako said,
    "All I have left
     are my bow and arrows
     and my *hadti,"*
which was her flint knife
and the *Estrucuyu* said,
     "Well you better give them to me,"
and so she handed over
her arrows and bows and her flint knife.
And about this time
Kochininako started to get scared
because whenever she gave the giant anything
he just took it
and he still didn't go away
he just asked for more.
"What else do you have to give me,"
he said.
"All I have left are my clothes."
"Well give them to me,"
he said.
Kochininako saw this sand rock cave nearby—
it was only one of those shallow caves—
but she saw it was her only chance

so she said,
"All right, you can have my clothes
but first I must go inside that cave over there
while I take them off."
The *Estrucuyu* wasn't very smart
and he didn't see right away
that his big head
would not fit through
the cave opening.
So he let her go
and Kochininako ran into the cave
and she got back as far as she could
in the cave
and she started taking off her clothes.
First she took off
her buckskin leggings
and threw them out of the cave
then she took off her moccasins
and threw them out the entrance to the cave.
She untied her belt
and threw it out to the giant.
Finally
all she had left
was her *manta* dress
and a short cotton smock underneath.
She took off her *manta*
and threw it out
to the *Estrucuyu*

and she told him
she didn't have anything more.
That was when
the *Estrucuyu*
started after her
poking his giant hand
into the cave
trying to grab hold of her
Kochininako moved fast
and kept getting away
but she knew
sooner or later
that old *Estrucuyu* would reach her.
So she started calling
for the Twin Brothers,
the Hero brothers,
Ma'see'wi and *Ou'yu'ye'wi*
who were always out
helping people who were in danger.
The Twin brothers
were fast runners
and she called them
and in no time
they were there.
Ma'see'wi and Ou'yu'ye'wi carry bows and arrows
and they each carry a flint knife
a "hadti"
like the one Kochininako carried for hunting.

86

When they got there
the *Estrucuyu* was scratching around
the entrance to the cave
trying to get Kochininako.
So the Twin brothers
each threw their *hadti*
their flint knives,
at the old *Estrucuyu*
and cut off his head—
that's how they killed him—
and they split open his stomach
and pulled out his heart
and they threw it
as far as they could throw—
they threw *Estrucuyu's* heart
clear across—
those things could happen
in those days—
and it landed right over here
near the river
between Laguna and Paguate
where the road turns to go
by the railroad tracks
right around
from John Paisano's place—
that big rock there
looks just like a heart,
and so his heart rested there

and that's why
it is called
Yash'ka
which means "heart."

23

Grandpa Stagner had a wagon and team and water drilling rig.
He traveled all over New Mexico drilling wells and putting up
or fixing windmills. In Los Lunas he had married
my great-grandmother, a granddaughter of the Romero family.
We called her Grandma Helen but even as a very young child
I sensed she did not like children much and so I remember her
from a distance, a tiny woman dressed in black, rolling her own
cigarettes in brown wheat papers. Grandma Lillie tells me
she spoke English but I remember Grandma Helen
speaking only Spanish when I was around her.
It was old Juana who had been like a mother to them.
It was old Juana who raised Grandma Lillie and her sisters
and brothers while Grandma Helen was in bed
either recovering from a birth or preparing for another one
in the genteel tradition of the Romero family.
Juana was already old when she came to work for them
and she lived with them until she died.
But when she had been just a little girl

Juana had been kidnapped by slavehunters
who attacked her family as they were traveling near Cubero.

Slavery of Navajo people went on in territorial New Mexico
until 1900.
The details are sketchy but by the time the territorial governor
made one of his half-hearted crackdowns on Indian slavery
Juana was an adult.
She spoke only Spanish
and no trace of her family remained.
So she continued with the work she knew
and years later Grandpa Stagner hired her
to help with the children.

On Memorial Day when I was a girl
Grandma Lillie and I always took flowers
to Juana's grave in the old graveyard behind the village.
The markers in the old graveyard are small flat sandstones
and many of them have been broken or covered with sand
and Grandma Lillie was never quite sure if we had found her grave
but we left the jar of roses and lilacs we had cut anyway.

🏵

His wife had caught them together before
and probably she had been hearing rumors again
the way people talk.

It was early August
after the corn was tall
and it was so hot in the afternoon
everyone just rested after lunch
or took naps
waiting for evening when it cools off
and you can go back to weeding
and working in the fields again.

That's what they were counting on—
this man and that woman—
they were going to wait
until everybody else went
back up to the village for lunch
then they were going to get together
down there in the corn fields.
That other woman was married too
but her husband was working in California.
This man's wife was always
watching him real close at night
so afternoon was
the only chance they had.

So anyway
they got together there
on the sandy ground between the rows of corn
where it's shady and cool
and the wind rattles the big corn stalks.

They were deep into those places where people go
when this man's wife showed up.
She suspected she would find them together
so she brought her two sisters along.
The two of them jumped up
and started putting their clothes back on
while his wife and his sisters-in-law
were standing there
saying all kinds of things
the way they do
how everyone in the village knows
and that's the worst thing.

So that other woman left
and it was just this poor man alone
with his wife and his sisters-in-law
and his wife would cry a little
and her sisters would say
                    "Don't cry, sister, don't cry,"
and then they would start talking again
about how good their family had treated him
and how lucky he was.

He couldn't look at them
so he looked at the sky
and then over at the hills behind the village.
They were talking now
what a fool he was

91

because that woman had a younger boyfriend
and it was only afternoons that she had any use
for an old man.

So pretty soon he started hoeing weeds again
because they were ignoring him
like he didn't matter anyway
now that
that woman was gone.

Then there was the night
old man George was going
down the hill to the toilet
and he heard strange sounds
coming from one of the old barns
below.
So he thought he better
check on things
just in case some poor animal
was trapped inside—
maybe somebody's cat.
So he shined his flashlight inside
and there was Frank—
so respectable and hard-working
and hardly ever drunk—
well there he was
naked with that Garcia girl—

you know,
the big fat one.
And here it was
the middle of winter
without their clothes on!

Poor old man George
he didn't know what to say
so he just closed the door again
and walked back home—
he even forgot where he was going
in the first place.

23

Grandma A'mooh had a worn-out little book that had lost its cover.
She used to read the book to me and my sisters
and later on I found out she'd read it to my uncles and my father.
We all remember Brownie the Bear
and she read the book to us again and again
and still we wanted to hear it.
Maybe it was because
she always read the story with such animation and expression
changing her tone of voice and inflection
each time one of the bears spoke—
the way a storyteller would have told it.

STORYTELLING

You should understand
the way it was
back then,
because it is the same
even now.

Long ago it happened
that her husband left
to hunt deer
before dawn
And then she got up
and went to get water.
Early in the morning
she walked to the river
when the sun came over
the long red mesa.

He was waiting for her
that morning
in the tamarack and willow
beside the river.

Buffalo Man
in buffalo leggings.
"Are you here already?"
"Yes," he said.
He was smiling.
"Because I came for you."
She looked into the
shallow clear water.
"But where shall I put my water jar?"
"Upside down, right here," he told her,
"on the river bank."

"You better have a damn good story,"
her husband said,
"about where you been for the past
ten months and how you explain these
twin baby boys."

"No! That gossip isn't true.
She didn't elope
She was *kidnapped* by
that Mexican
at Seama feast.

You know
my daughter
isn't
that kind of girl."

It was
in the summer
of 1967.
T.V. news reported
a kidnapping.
Four Laguna women
and three Navajo men
headed north along
the Rio Puerco river
in a red '56 Ford
and the F.B.I. and
state police were
hot on their trail
of wine bottles and
size 42 panties
hanging in bushes and trees
all along the road.

"We couldn't escape them," he told police later.
"We tried, but there were four of them and
only three of us."

Seems like
it's always happening to me.
Outside the dance hall door
late Friday night
in the summertime,
and those
brown-eyed men from Cubero,
smiling.
They usually ask me
"Have you seen the way stars shine
up there in the sand hills?"
And I usually say "No. Will you show me?"

It was
that Navajo
from Alamo,
you know,
the tall
good-looking
one.

He told me
he'd kill me

if I didn't
go with him
And then it
rained so much
and the roads
got muddy.
That's why
it took me
so long
to get back home.

My husband
left
after he heard the story
and moved back in with his mother.
It was my fault and
I don't blame him either.
I could have told
the story
better than I did.

THE TWO SISTERS

Ahsti-ey and Hait-ti-eh were two girls,
pueblo girls who lived in Hani-a.
Hani-a was supposed to be
traditionally, Cienega,
you know where Cienega is
the place between Albuquerque and Santa Fe.
They called it "Hania"
that means, interpreted,
"the East Country."
It is east from here.
It means the "East Country," yes.
The two sisters
they were Hait-ti-eh
and Ahsti-ey—
those were their names.
They were interested in a young man
by the name of Estoy-eh-muut.
"Muut" means "youth."
"Estoyeh" means that he was a great hunter.
And they were both interested in this young man
and they were trying to see
who would finally win him over
on her side.
Ahsti-ey was beautiful.
So was Hait-ti-eh.

100

Hait-ti-eh had beautiful hair,
beautiful hair, the sister did.
And Estoy-eh-muut would come to visit them.
As he came
he would bring venison.
You know that is the original food, venison is.
The pueblo people have always depended upon it
depended on the deer for food.
So Estoy-eh-muut came quite often
and he would bring meat
from the deer he hunted.
Finally Ahsti-ey suspected something—
that Estoy-eh-muut thought more of her sister, Hait-ti-eh,
the one who had beautiful long hair.
So there was jealousy right away
it developed in Ahsti-ey
and she was just wondering how
she could ward off
Estoy-eh-muut's devotion to her sister, Hait-ti-eh
which was much more than he gave to her.
So now anything can take place
in the story. . . .
So one evening
the girls went to bed
and she thought of trickery
that she would play on Hait-ti-eh,
the one who had beautiful hair.

So Ahsti-ey called mice in
that evening
and had the mice eat
all of Hait-ti-eh's hair
and that spoiled her looks,
of course.
And so when Estoy-eh-muut, the young hunter, came,
he saw that Hait-ti-eh's beautiful hair was gone,
but still
that didn't deter him
from thinking much of her, Hait-ti-eh.
So he kept coming.
The story is told in a song.
Many of these stories
sometimes end up in songs.
This story is found in one of the grinding songs.
The grinding song belonged
to the Ka-shalee clan,
and so the story is related in this song
and it tells that something tragic
took place in those far-off days.
The tragedy was
that Hait-ti-eh's hair was all gone.
The end of the song goes like this:

                    Long ago
                            in the East Country
                    called Tse'dihania
                    this took place

something tragic took place.
So the people migrated from there.
The people of Ahsti-ey and Hait-ti-eh
came to Laguna
and settled here
because something tragic took place.

OUT OF THE WORKS NO GOOD COMES FROM

Possession

It will come to you
late one night
distinctly
while your wife
waits in bed.
You will reach into pockets
for something you feel is missing
a key, perhaps silver coins, a leather wallet.
Folded pieces of paper are still within reach
but the feeling now
is overwhelming
of something no longer with you.

You walk outside
in the dark
feel for the gloves
on the seat of your truck.

Something has been left behind,
something has been lost.

All night in bed beside her
your heart pounds out
possible locations
for a loss so complete
even its name has escaped you.
At dawn she turns in bed and
you see from your place in the bed
the impossibility of this
her hair spreads over your pillow
her arms where yours are resting.
Listen now
before you make any sudden move
for your breathing
which once accompanied you.

Incantation

The television
lights up the room,
a continual presence.
Seconds minutes
flicker in gray intervals
on the wall beside my head.
Even if

104

I could walk to the window
I would only see
gray video images
bending against the clouds.

At one time
more might have been necessary—
            a smokey quartz crystal
            balanced in the center of the palm—
But tonight
there is enough.

The simple equation you found
in my notebook
frightened you
but I could have explained it:
            After all bright colors of sunset and
            leaves are added together
            lovers are subtracted
            children multiplied, are divided, taken away.
The remainder is small enough
to stay in this room forever
gray-shadowing restless
trapped on a gray glass plain.

I did not plan to tell you.
Better to lose colors gradually

first the blue of the eyes
then the red of blood
its salt taste fading
water gone suddenly bitter
when the last yellow light
blinks off the screen.

Wherever you're heading tonight
you think you're leaving me
                 and the equation of this gray room.
Hold her close
    pray
        these are lies I'm telling you.

As with the set which lost its color
and only hums gray outlines,
it is a matter of intensity and hue
and the increasing distance—
The interval will grow as imperceptibly
as it grew between us.

You'll drive on
putting distance and time between us—
        the snow in the high Sierras
        the dawn along the Pacific
dreaming you've left this narrow room.

But tonight
I have traced all escape routes
with my finger across the t.v. weather map.
        Your ocean dawn is only the gray light
           in the corner of this room
       Your mountain snowstorm
          flies against the glass screen
          until we both are buried.

     A Note

They tell you
they try to warn you
about some particular cliff
sandrock a peculiar cloudy dawn color.

It is the place,
         they say
where so many others have fallen.
Remember Chemí's son?
So handsome—
What was it
he wanted up there?

She only came from that direction
one time

and so long ago
no one living
ever heard anyone tell
they saw her.

Don't go looking
don't even raise your eyes.

Saturday morning I was walking past Nora's house
and she was outside building a fire in her oven.
I stopped to say hello and we were talking and
she said her grandchildren had brought home
a library book that had my "Laguna Coyote" poem in it.
              "We all enjoyed it so much,
                but I was telling the children
                the way my grandpa used to tell it
                is longer."
"Yes, that's the trouble with writing," I said,
  "You can't go on and on the way we do
  when we tell stories around here.
  People who aren't used to it get tired."

              "I remember Grandpa telling us that story—
                We would *really* laugh!
                He wouldn't begin until we gave him
                something real good to eat—
                roasted piñons or some jerky.
                Then he would start telling the story.
                That's what you're supposed to do, you know, ′
                you're supposed to feed the storyteller good things."

110

One time
Old Woman Ck'o'yo's
son came in
from Reedleaf town
up north.
His name was Pa'caya'nyi
and he didn't know who his father was.

He asked the people
"You people want to learn some magic?"
and the people said
"Yes, we can always use some."

Ma'see'wi and Ou'yu'ye'wi
the Twin Brothers
were caring for the
Mother Corn altar,
but they got interested
in this magic too.

"What kind of medicine man
are you,
anyway?" they asked him.
"A Ck'o'yo medicine man,"
he said.

111

"Tonight we'll see
if you really have magical power," they told him.

So that night
Pa'caya'nyi
came with his mountain lion.
He undressed
he painted his body
the whorls of flesh
the soles of his feet
the palms of his hands
the top of his head.

He wore feathers
on each side of his head.

He made an altar
with cactus spines
and purple locoweed flowers.
He lighted four cactus torches
at each corner.
He made the mountain lion lie
down in front and
then he was ready for his magic.

He struck the middle of the north wall
He took a piece of flint and
he struck the middle of the north wall.

Water poured out of the wall
and flowed down
toward the south.
He said "What does that look like?
Is that magic powers?"
He struck the middle of the west wall
and from the east wall
a bear came out.
"What do you call this?"
he said again.

"Yes, it looks like magic all right,"
Ma'see'wi said.
So it was finished
and Ma'see'wi and Ou'yu'ye'wi
and all the people were fooled by
that Ck'o'yo medicine man,
Pa'caya'nyi.

From that time on
they were
so busy
playing around with that
Ck'o'yo magic
they neglected the Mother Corn altar.

They thought they didn't have to worry
about anything.

They thought this magic
could give life to plants
and animals.
They didn't know it was all just a trick.

Our mother
Nau'ts'ity'i
was very angry
over this
over the way
all of them
even Ma'see'wi and Ou'yu'ye'wi
fooled around with this
magic.

"I've had enough of that,"
she said,
"If they like that magic so much
let them live off it."

So she took
the plants and grass from them.
No baby animals were born.
She took the
rain clouds with her.

The wind stirred the dust.
The people were starving.

"She's angry with us,"
the people said.
"Maybe because of that
Ck'o'yo magic
we were fooling with.
We better send someone
to ask our forgiveness."

They noticed Hummingbird
was fat and shiny
he had plenty to eat.
They asked how come he
looked so good.

He said
Down below
Three worlds below this one
everything is
green
all the plants are growing
the flowers are blooming.
I go down there
and eat.

"So that's where our mother went.
How can we get down there?"

Hummingbird looked at all the
skinny people.

He felt sorry for them.
He said, "You need a messenger.
Listen, I'll tell you
what to do":

Bring a beautiful pottery jar
painted with parrots and big
flowers.
Mix black mountain dirt
some sweet corn flour
and a little water.

Cover the jar with a
new buckskin
and say this over the jar
and sing this softly
above the jar:

After four days
you will be alive
After four days
you will be alive
After four days
you will be alive
After four days
you will be alive.

On the fourth day
something buzzed around
inside the jar.

They lifted the buckskin
and a big green fly
with yellow feelers on his head
flew out of the jar.

"Fly will go with me," Hummingbird said.
"We'll go see
what she wants."

They flew to the fourth world
below.
Down there
was another kind of daylight
everything was blooming
and growing
everything was so beautiful.

Fly started sucking on
sweet things so
Hummingbird had to tell him
to wait:
"Wait until we see our Mother."
They found her.

They gave her blue pollen and yellow pollen
they gave her turquoise beads
they gave her prayer sticks.

"I suppose you want something," she said.
"Yes, we want food and storm clouds."
"You get old Buzzard to purify
your town first
and then, maybe, I will send you people
food and rain again."

Fly and Hummingbird
flew back up.
They told the town people
that old Buzzard had to purify
the town.

They took more pollen,
more beads, and more prayer sticks,
and they went to see old Buzzard.

They arrived at his place in the east.
"Who's out there?
Nobody ever came here before."
"It's us, Hummingbird and Fly."
"Oh. What do you want?"
"We need you to purify our town."

"Well, look here. Your offering isn't
complete. Where's the tobacco?"

You see, it wasn't easy.
Fly and Hummingbird
had to fly back to town again.

The people asked,
"Did you find him?"
"Yes, but we forgot something.
Tobacco."
But there was no tobacco
so Fly and Hummingbird had to fly
all the way back down
to the fourth world below
to ask our Mother where
they could get some tobacco.

"We came back again,"
they told our Mother.
"Maybe you need something?"
"Tobacco."
"Go ask caterpillar."

So they flew
all the way up again.
They went to a place in the West.

See, these things were complicated. . . .
They called outside his house
"You downstairs, how are things?"
"Okay," he said, "come down."
They went down inside.
"Maybe you want something?"
"Yes. We need tobacco."
Caterpillar spread out
dry cornhusks on the floor.
He rubbed his hands together
and tobacco fell into the cornhusks.
Then he folded up the husks
and gave the tobacco to them.

Hummingbird and Fly thanked him.
They took the tobacco to old Buzzard.
"Here it is. We finally got it but it
sure wasn't very easy."
"Okay," Buzzard said.
"Go back and tell them
I'll purify the town."

And he did—
first to the east
then to the south
then to the west
and finally to the north.

Everything was set straight again
after all that Ck'o'yo magic.

The storm clouds returned
the grass and plants started growing again.
There was food
and the people were happy again.

So she told them
"Stay out of trouble
from now on.

It isn't very easy
to fix up things again.
Remember that
next time
some Ck'o'yo magician
comes to town."

POEM FOR MYSELF AND MEI: *Concerning Abortion*

Chinle to Fort Defiance, April 1973

The morning sun
        coming unstuffed with yellow light
        butterflies tumbling loose
        and blowing across the Earth.
They fill the sky
        with shimmering yellow wind
        and I see them with the clarity of ice
        shattered in mountain streams
                where each pebble is
                speckled and marbled
                alive beneath the water.

All winter it snowed
mustard grass
and springtime rained it.

Wide fancy meadows
warm green
        and butterflies are yellow mustard flowers
                spilling out of the mountain.

There were horses
     near the highway
     at Ganado.
And the white one
       scratching his ass on a tree.

They die softly
against the windshield
and the iridescent wings
     flutter and cling
       all the way home.

TONY'S STORY

It happened one summer when the sky was wide and hot and the summer rains did not come; the sheep were thin, and the tumbleweeds turned brown and died. Leon came back from the army. I saw him standing by the Ferris wheel across from the people who came to sell melons and chili on San Lorenzo's Day. He yelled at me, "Hey Tony—over here!" I was embarrassed to hear him yell so loud, but then I saw the wine bottle with the brown-paper sack crushed around it.

"How's it going, buddy?"

123

He grabbed my hand and held it tight like a white man. He was smiling. "It's good to be home again. They asked me to dance tomorrow—it's only the Corn Dance, but I hope I haven't forgotten what to do."

"You'll remember—it will all come back to you when you hear the drum." I was happy, because I knew that Leon was once more a part of the pueblo. The sun was dusty and low in the west, and the procession passed by us, carrying San Lorenzo back to his niche in the church.

"Do you want to get something to eat?" I asked.

Leon laughed and patted the bottle. "No, you're the only one who needs to eat. Take this dollar—they're selling hamburgers over there." He pointed past the merry-go-round to a stand with cotton candy and a snow-cone machine.

It was then that I saw the cop pushing his way through the crowds of people gathered around the hamburger stand and bingo tent; he came steadily toward us. I remembered Leon's wine and looked to see if the cop was watching us; but he was wearing dark glasses and I couldn't see his eyes.

He never said anything before he hit Leon in the face with his fist. Leon collapsed into the dust, and the paper sack floated in the wine and pieces of glasses. He didn't move and blood kept bubbling out of his mouth and nose. I could hear a siren. People crowded around Leon and kept pushing me away. The tribal policemen knelt over Leon, and one of them looked up at the state cop and asked what was going on. The big cop didn't answer. He was staring at the little patterns of blood in the dust near Leon's mouth. The dust soaked up the blood almost before it dripped to the ground—it had been a very dry summer. The cop didn't leave until they laid Leon in the back of the paddy wagon.

The moon was already high when we got to the hospital in Albuquerque. We waited a long time outside the emergency room with Leon propped between us. Siow and Gaisthea kept asking me, "What happened, what did Leon say to the cop?" and I told them how we were just standing there, ready to buy hamburgers—we'd never even seen him before.

They put stitches around Leon's mouth and gave him a shot; he was lucky, they said—it could've been a broken jaw instead of broken teeth.

———

They dropped me off near my house. The moon had moved lower into the west and left the close rows of houses in long shadows. Stillness breathed around me, and I wanted to run from the feeling behind me in the dark; and the stories about witches ran with me. That night I had a dream—the big cop was pointing a long bone at me—they always use human bones, and the whiteness flashed silver in the moonlight where he stood. He didn't have a human face—only little, round, white-rimmed eyes on a black ceremonial mask.

Leon was better in a few days. But he was bitter, and all he could talk about was the cop. "I'll kill the big bastard if he comes around here again," Leon kept saying.

With something like the cop it is better to forget, and I tried to make Leon understand. "It's over now. There's nothing you can do."

I wondered why men who came back from the army were troublemakers on the reservation. Leon even took it before the pueblo meeting. They discussed it, and the old men decided that Leon shouldn't have been drinking. The interpreter read a passage out of the revised pueblo law-and-order code about possessing intoxicants on the reservation, so we got up and left.

Then Leon asked me to go with him to Grants to buy a roll of barbed wire for his uncle. On the way we stopped at Cerritos for gas, and I went into the store for some pop. He was inside. I stopped in the doorway and turned around before he saw me, but if he really was what I feared, then he would not need to see me—he already knew we were there. Leon was waiting with the truck engine running almost like he knew what I would say.

"Let's go—the big cop's inside."

Leon gunned it and the pickup skidded back on the highway. He glanced back in the rearview mirror. "I didn't see his car."

"Hidden," I said.

Leon shook his head. "He can't do it again. We are just as good as them."

The guys who came back always talked like that.

The sky was hot and empty. The half-grown tumbleweeds were dried up flat and brown beside the highway, and across the valley, heat shimmered above wilted fields of corn. Even the mountains high beyond the pale sandrock mesas were dusty blue. I was afraid to fall asleep so I kept my eyes on the blue mountains—not letting them close—soaking in the heat; and then I knew why the drought had come that summer.

Leon shook me. "He's behind us—the cop's following us!"

I looked back and saw the red light on top of the car whirling around, and I could make out the dark image of a man, but where the face should have been there were only the silvery lenses of the dark glasses he wore.

"Stop, Leon! He wants us to stop!"

Leon pulled over and stopped on the narrow gravel shoulder.

"What in the hell does he want?" Leon's hands were shaking.

Suddenly the cop was standing beside the truck, gesturing for Leon to roll down his window. He pushed his head inside, grinding the gum in his mouth; the smell of Doublemint was all around us.

"Get out. Both of you."

I stood beside Leon in the dry weeds and tall yellow grass that broke through the asphalt and rattled in the wind. The cop studied Leon's driver's license. I avoided his face—I knew that I couldn't look at his eyes, so I stared at his black half-Wellingtons, with the black uniform cuffs pulled over them; but my eyes kept moving, up-ward past the black gun belt. My legs were quivering, and I tried to keep my eyes away from his. But it was like the time when I was very little and my parents warned me not to look into the masked dancers' eyes because they would grab me, and my eyes would not stop.

"What's your name?" His voice was high-pitched and it distracted me from the meaning of the words.

I remember Leon said, "He doesn't understand English so good," and finally I said that I was Antonio Sousea, while my eyes strained to look beyond the silver frosted glasses that he wore; but only my distorted face and squinting eyes reflected back.

And then the cop stared at us for a while, silent; finally he laughed and chewed his gum some more slowly. "Where were you going?"

"To Grants." Leon spoke English very clearly. "Can we go now?"

Leon was twisting the key chain around his fingers, and I felt the sun everywhere. Heat swelled up from the asphalt and when cars went by, hot air and the motor smell rushed past us.

"I don't like smart guys, Indian. It's because of you bastards that I'm here. They transferred me here because of Indians. They thought there wouldn't be as many for me here. But I find them." He spit his gum into the weeds near my foot and walked back to the patrol car. It kicked up gravel and dust when he left.

We got back in the pickup, and I could taste sweat in my mouth, so I told Leon that we might as well go home since he would be waiting for us up ahead.

"He can't do this," Leon said. "We've got a right to be on this highway."

I couldn't understand why Leon kept talking about "rights," because it wasn't "rights" that he was after, but Leon didn't seem to understand; he couldn't remember the stories that old Teofilo told.

I didn't feel safe until we turned off the highway and I could see the pueblo and my own house. It was noon, and everybody was eating—the village seemed empty—even the dogs had crawled away from the heat. The door was open, but there was only silence, and I was afraid that something had happened to all of them. Then as soon as I opened the screen door the little kids started crying for more Kool-Aid, and my mother said "no," and it was noisy again like always. Grandfather commented that it had been a fast trip to Grants, and I said "yeah" and didn't explain because it would've only worried them.

"Leon goes looking for trouble—I wish you wouldn't hang around with him." My father didn't like trouble. But I knew that the cop was something terrible, and even to speak about it risked bringing it close to all of us; so I didn't say anything.

That afternoon Leon spoke with the Governor, and he promised to send letters to the Bureau of Indian Affairs and to the State Police Chief. Leon seemed satisfied with that. I reached into my pocket for the arrowhead on the piece of string.

"What's that for?"

I held it out to him. "Here, wear it around your neck—like mine. See? Just in case," I said, "for protection."

"You don't believe in *that*, do you?" He pointed to a .30-30 leaning against the wall. "I'll take this with me whenever I'm in the pickup."

"But you can't be sure that it will kill one of them."

Leon looked at me and laughed. "What's the matter," he said, "have they brainwashed you into believing that a .30-30 won't kill a white man?" He handed back the arrowhead. "Here, you wear two of them."

———

127

Leon's uncle asked me if I wanted to stay at the sheep camp for a while. The lambs were big, and there wouldn't be much for me to do, so I told him I would. We left early, while the sun was still low and red in the sky. The highway was empty, and I sat there beside Leon imagining what it had been like before there were highways or even horses. Leon turned off the highway onto the sheep-camp road that climbs around the sandstone mesas until suddenly all the trees are piñons.

Leon glanced in the rearview mirror. "He's following us!"

My body began to shake and I wasn't sure if I would be able to speak. "There's no place left to hide. It follows us everywhere."

Leon looked at me like he didn't understand what I'd said. Then I looked past Leon and saw that the patrol car had pulled up beside us; the piñon branches were whipping and scraping the side of the truck as it tried to force us off the road. Leon kept driving with the two right wheels in the rut—bumping and scraping the trees. Leon never looked over at it so he couldn't have known how the reflections kept moving across the mirror lenses of the dark glasses. We were in the narrow canyon with pale sandstone close on either side— the canyon that ended with a spring where willows and grass and tiny blue flowers grow.

"We've got to kill it, Leon. We must burn the body to be sure."

Leon didn't seem to be listening. I kept wishing that old Teofilo could have been there to chant the proper words while we did it. Leon stopped the truck and got out—he still didn't understand what it was. I sat in the pickup with the .30–30 across my lap, and my hands were slippery.

The big cop was standing in front of the pickup, facing Leon. "You made your mistake, Indian. I'm going to beat the shit out of you." He raised the billy club slowly. "I like to beat Indians with this."

He moved toward Leon with the stick raised high, and it was like the long bone in my dream when he pointed it at me—a human bone painted brown to look like wood, to hide what it really was; they'll do that, you know—carve the bone into a spoon and use it around the house until the victim comes within range.

The shot sounded far away and I couldn't remember aiming. But he was motionless on the ground and the bone wand lay near his feet. The tumbleweeds and tall yellow grass were sprayed with glossy, bright blood. He was on his back, and the sand between his legs and along his left side was soaking up the dark, heavy blood—it had not rained for a long time, and even the tumbleweeds were dying.

"Tony! You killed him—you killed the cop!"

"Help me! We'll set the car on fire."

Leon acted strange, and he kept looking at me like he wanted to run. The head wobbled and swung back and forth, and the left hand and the legs left individual trails in the sand. The face was the same. The dark glasses hadn't fallen off and they blinded me with their hot-sun reflections until I pushed the body into the front seat.

The gas tank exploded and the flames spread along the underbelly of the car. The tires filled the wide sky with spirals of thick black smoke.

"My God, Tony. What's wrong with you? That's a state cop you killed." Leon was pale and shaking.

I wiped my hands on my Levi's. "Don't worry, everything is O.K. now, Leon. It's killed. They sometimes take on strange forms."

The tumbleweeds around the car caught fire, and little heat waves shimmered up toward the sky; in the west, rain clouds were gathering.

Long time ago
in the beginning
there were no white people in this world
there was nothing European.
And this world might have gone on like that
except for one thing:
witchery.
This world was already complete
even without white people.
There was everything
including witchery.

Then it happened.
These witch people got together.
Some came from far far away
across oceans
across mountains.
Some had slanty eyes
others had black skin.
They all got together for a contest
the way people have baseball tournaments nowadays
except this was a contest
in dark things.

130

So anyway
they all got together
witch people from all directions
witches from all the Pueblos
and all the tribes.
They had Navajo witches there,
some from Hopi, and a few from Zuni.
They were having a witches' conference,
that's what it was
Way up in the lava rock hills
north of Cañoncito
they got together
to fool around in caves
with their animal skins.
Fox, badger, bobcat, and wolf
they circled the fire
and on the fourth time
they jumped into that animal's skin.

But this time it wasn't enough
and one of them
maybe a Sioux or some Eskimos
started showing off.
"That wasn't anything,
watch this."

The contest started like that.
Then some of them lifted the lids

on their big cooking pots,
calling the rest of them over
to take a look:
dead babies simmering in blood
circles of skull cut away
all the brains sucked out.
Witch medicine
to dry and grind into powder
for new victims.

Others untied skin bundles of disgusting objects:
dark flints, cinders from burned hogans where the
dead lay
Whorls of skin
cut from fingertips
sliced from the penis end and clitoris tip.

Finally there was only one
who hadn't shown off charms or powers.
The witch stood in the shadows beyond the fire
and no one ever knew where this witch came from
which tribe
or if it was a woman or a man.
But the important thing was
this witch didn't show off any dark thunder charcoals
or red ant-hill beads.
This one just told them to listen:
"What I have is a story."

At first they all laughed
but this witch said
Okay
go ahead
laugh if you want to
but as I tell the story
it will begin to happen.

Set in motion now
set in motion by our witchery
to work for us.

Caves across the ocean
in caves of dark hills
white skin people
like the belly of a fish
covered with hair.

Then they grow away from the earth
then they grow away from the sun
then they grow away from the plants and animals.
They see no life
When they look
they see only objects.
The world is a dead thing for them
the trees and rivers are not alive
the mountains and stones are not alive.
The deer and bear are objects
They see no life.

133

They fear
They fear the world.
They destroy what they fear.
They fear themselves.

The wind will blow them across the ocean
thousands of them in giant boats
swarming like larva
out of a crushed ant hill.

They will carry objects
which can shoot death
faster than the eye can see.

They will kill the things they fear
all the animals
the people will starve.

They will poison the water
they will spin the water away
and there will be drought
the people will starve.

They will fear what they find
They will fear the people
They kill what they fear.

Entire villages will be wiped out
They will slaughter whole tribes.

Corpses for us
Blood for us
Killing killing killing killing.

And those they do not kill
will die anyway
at the destruction they see
at the loss
at the loss of the children
the loss will destroy the rest.

Stolen rivers and mountains
the stolen land will eat their hearts
and jerk their mouths from the Mother.
The people will starve.

They will bring terrible diseases
the people have never known.
Entire tribes will die out
covered with festered sores
shitting blood
vomiting blood.
Corpses for our work

Set in motion now
set in motion by our witchery
set in motion
to work for us.

They will take this world from ocean to ocean
they will turn on each other
they will destroy each other
Up here
in these hills
they will find the rocks,
rocks with veins of green and yellow and black.
They will lay the final pattern with these rocks
they will lay it across the world
and explode everything.

Set in motion now
set in motion
To destroy
To kill
Objects to work for us
objects to act for us
Performing the witchery
for suffering
for torment
for the stillborn
the deformed
the sterile
the dead.

Whirling
Whirling
Whirling

Whirling
set into motion now
set into motion.

So the other witches said
"Okay you win; you take the prize,
but what you said just now—
it isn't so funny
It doesn't sound so good.
We are doing okay without it
we can get along without that kind of thing.
Take it back.
Call that story back."

But the witch just shook its head
at the others in their stinking animal skins, fur
and feathers.
It's already turned loose.
It's already coming.
It can't be called back.

ESTOY-EH-MUUT AND THE KUNIDEEYAHS

Estoy-eh-muut, Arrowboy, had not been married
very long before he started to feel
something was not as it should be.
Something felt out of place
but he didn't know what it was.

At first he thought
it must be the long hours
spent in his fields
the worry over the drought
and the spring that went dry.

But one evening
when he was visiting his parents
his sister asked
who had been sick at his house
the night before.

"No one," Estoy-eh-muut told her.
"I saw someone last night,"
his sister told him,
"when I got up with the baby—I happened to look
across the plaza and I saw someone
going out your door."

"You must have been dreaming," Estoy-eh-muut told her.
"I would have heard if anyone went out."

Days passed and still Estoy-eh-muut felt
something was out of place.
He slept all night
without dreaming
but in the morning he was exhausted.
As he worked in the fields
the heat made him dizzy and weak.

The corn plants had been sickly that year
and the worms devoured all the bean plants.

When he told his wife, Kochininako.
that he was afraid something was happening
she only laughed
and told him to get to bed earlier.
So he did
but the next morning
he went to see
old Spider Woman,
who always helped the people
whenever they faced great difficulties.

She was sitting under a snakeweed plant
near the entrance to her house.
"Oh you poor thing!" Spider Woman said
when she saw him.
"Have you been sick?
Come inside, rest awhile."

"How shall I get in?" Estoy-eh-muut asked.
"Your house is so small."

"Go ahead, put your foot in the door,"
she told him.
And when he did
he was able to enter
the spider hole

"What's wrong, Grandson?"
old Spider Woman asked him,
"Maybe I can help you."

"Something doesn't feel right, Grandmother,
I don't know what it is
but it seems to be getting worse all the time.
Especially in the morning
when I wake up—
that's when it is the worst—
a fear for all of us
that leaves me shaking the rest of the day.

"Then whatever it is
it happens at night
while you are asleep," Spider Woman told him.
"Here, my dear grandson,
take this special powder.

Swallow it

before you go to bed.
The powder will keep you
awake
but I want you to pretend
you are sleeping.
Don't tell anyone
not even Kochininako.
Wait.
See what happens."

So that night
he swallowed the medicine
old Spider Woman had given him
and he went to bed
and pretended to sleep.

Kochininako came to bed soon after
but he could tell
by the sound of her breathing
she was not asleep.
When she touched his shoulder
he did not move.

She got up then
and silently left the room
but she returned
and placed something in the bed
beside him.

"Dark purple corn,"
Kochininako said softly,
"Keep Estoy-eh-muut asleep
while I am gone.
Don't let him awake
until I return."

The ear of dark purple corn
had the power to make him sleep
but Spider Woman's medicine
protected Estoy-eh-muut from it
that night.

He listened
he could hear Kochininako lift the lid
on the cooking pot.
He could hear her bundling up something.
Then she left the house
carrying food with her.

Estoy-eh-muut followed her
wondering where Kochininako was going
in the middle of the night.
He followed her north
far from the village
to a place in the hills
where there are many caves
144   in the sandstone cliffs.

He could smell woodsmoke
then he could see the dim light
from a fire inside a large shallow cave.
Kochininako stepped inside.

As Estoy-eh-muut crept closer
he could hear the hollow sound
of human voices inside the cave.

Then he knew:
She was a secret member
of the Kunideeyah Clan.
Kochininako was going to a meeting
of the Kunideeyah,
the Destroyers.

"Kochininako, our sister,"
they greeted her
"You are late tonight."

"Yes," he heard Kochininako answer
"Estoy-eh-muut took a long time
getting to sleep."

"Let's go ahead with our meeting,"
the leader of the Kunideeyah said.
"Each one of you will go under
this cottonwood bow and say
which animal form you want to take."

"I want to be a bear,"
the first one said
going under the cottonwood bow.
"I want to be a crow,"
said the second one.

Nothing happened.
"Something is wrong,"
the leader said.
"Kochininako, go and see
if an outsider is spying on us."

Kochininako went out
as she was ordered and
there she found Estoy-eh-muut,
her husband,
creeping around the cave.
This was why the magic
had not worked.

"Estoy-eh-muut is out there,"
she told them.
"Well, take Estoy-eh-muut home,"
they told her.
This time she had a broom straw
in her hand
she said "Broom straw!
Broom straw put Estoy-eh-muut to sleep!"

And as she spoke
Estoy-eh-muut felt suddenly tired
and though he tried to fight it
he fell asleep.

Kochininako took her sleeping husband
to the cliff
a dangerous and precipitous cliff
nearby.
The cliff was called
                    "Mah'de'haths"
the place of no escape.
She laid him on the narrow edge
and returned to her meeting.

The members of the Kunideeyah Clan
went under the cottonwood bow
changing into animal forms
now that there was no one
to interfere with the magic.

Then the Kunideeyahs went
to perform their night work
uttering weird cries
of wolves, mountain lions, coyotes and bears.

The whip snake Kunideeyah crawled into a house
and left an ugly bundle

of human hair and excrement tied together
to cause madness in that house.

The bear Kunideeyah attacked
a lone night traveler from another pueblo
and dragged the body away.

Wearing wolfskin shirts
other Kunideeyahs
stampeded the deer from the hunting places
so the village people would go hungry.

The bull snake strangled a sleeping baby
and the coyote partner
carried the small corpse away
moving through the night
doing their work of destruction.

When they had completed their missions
the Kunideeyahs returned to the cave
and regained their human forms.

They feasted at midnight
on the heart of the slain traveler
and on the infant's brain.
When they had finished
they fell upon each other
men embracing other men

women reaching for the rattlesnake,
the whip snake Kunideeyahs
they desired.
They returned to their homes
before dawn.

Estoy-eh-muut woke up
on a ledge so narrow
he could not move in any direction.

"Oh my mother! Oh my sister!"
he cried,
"Kochininako has put me on the ledge
and I don't know how to get down!"

Two little ground squirrels heard his voice
coming from the cliff which is
impossible to reach.
They knew no person could reach
that ledge alive
so they became very frightened
thinking what they heard was
a dead person crying.
They ran home
and hid themselves in a pile of acorns
so that only their little bright eyes
peeked out.

When Old Mother Ground Squirrel came home
she asked why they were hiding.
They told her they heard a dead person
crying on the high cliff.

"Dead persons will never cry,"
she told her children,
"Let's go.
Probably the Kunideeyahs have left some
poor victim up there to die."

The ground squirrels went
to the foot of the high cliff
where they heard a voice crying
"Oh my mother! Oh my sister!
Kochininako has put me on this cliff
and I don't know how to get down!"

"Oh my poor grandson,"
the mother ground squirrel called
up to him,
"You must not move or you will fall.
I will get you down in four days."

"I'm so thirsty, Grandmother."
"You must bear your thirst, Grandson.
In four days
I will see that you get water."

Then the old ground squirrel planted
four piñon seeds
at the foot of the cliff.
She watered them everyday
and on the fourth day
the seeds had grown into tall piñon trees
reaching the ledge just where
Estoy-eh-muut lay.

Then the little ground squirrels carried
water in little acorn shell cups
up the piñon trees
to the ledge.
It took many acorn cups to satisfy
Estoy-eh-muut's thirst.

When he had regained his strength
he climbed down a piñon tree
and went home with the old ground squirrel
and her children.

Estoy-eh-muut was a great hunter
and he brought the family
many rabbits and deer.
After a long time there
he was ready to go home.

He had not traveled far
when he heard someone calling

"Grandson! Grandson! Over here!"
It was old Spider Woman
calling from her place
under a yucca.

"Estoy-eh-muut! Grandson!
Where are you going?"

"I'm going home,"
he told her,
"Kochininako belongs to the Kunideeyah Clan
and I must warn the people about her."

"Oh my dear Grandson.
You can't go home yet.
When Kochininako sees you did not die
on the cliff
she will try to kill you."

"But what can I do?"

"Remain here with me four days
while I prepare something
to protect you," Spider Woman told him.

So Estoy-eh-muut waited
while Spider Woman took yucca fiber

and began weaving a coiled ring
called a *maas-guuts*
used to cushion the water jars
the people carried
balanced on their heads.

As she wove it
an unusual design began to appear—
the figure of a snake.
On the fourth day
Grandmother Spider had completed
the small woven-coil ring
and she gave Estoy-eh-muut
the instructions:
"Now listen very carefully, Grandson
to what I say:

> You must not let
> Kochininako see you first or
> she will kill you.
> As soon as you see her—
>   quickly—
> roll this *maas-guuts*
> right at her!"

Estoy-eh-muut gave Spider Woman some
rabbits and a deer he had brought
and thanked her for all her help.

He approached the village
very carefully from the hill behind it.
He waited on the hill
and when he saw Kochininako come out
he rolled the woven coil down the hill
at her
the way Spider Woman had told him he must.

The coiled ring of
woven yucca fiber
went rolling straight to Kochininako
but when it hit her chest
it became a rattlesnake that struck her
and killed her.

16

17

THE GO-WA-PEU-ZI SONG:

      Hena-ti-tzi
      He-ya-she-tzi
      So-you-tano-mi-ha-ai
Of the clouds
and rain clouds
and growth of corn
I sing.

It was summertime
and Iktoa'ak'o'ya-Reed Woman
was always taking a bath.
She spent all day long
sitting in the river
splashing down
the summer rain.

But her sister
Corn Woman

worked hard all day
sweating in the sun
getting sore hands
in the corn field.
Corn Woman got tired of that
she got angry
she scolded
her sister
for bathing all day long.

Iktoa'ak'o'ya-Reed Woman
went away then
she went back
to the original place
down below.

And there was no more rain then.
Everything dried up
all the plants
the corn
the beans
they all dried up
and started blowing away
in the wind.

The people and the animals
were thirsty.
They were starving.

The hills and mesas around Laguna
were a second home for my father
when he was growing up.
He ran away from school for the hills
where he found less trouble.
When we were growing up
he took my sisters and me hiking and exploring
those same hills the way he had done when he was a boy.
He is still most at home in the canyons and sandrock
and most of his life regular jobs
have been a confinement he has avoided.
He used to wait for the cumulus clouds to come give him the sky
he needed for his photographs.
When I was a girl
I could tell by the clouds
whether I'd find him working at the store
or if he had grabbed his cameras
and told my grandpa he'd be right back
meaning he'd be gone all afternoon.

Sometimes I was there when the clouds came
and he'd tell me I could go but to hurry
get into the pickup
the clouds move through so fast.

His landscapes could not be done
without certain kinds of clouds—
       some white and scattered like river rock
       and others
       mountains rolling into themselves
       swollen lavender before rainstorms.
As I got older
he said I should become a writer
because writers worked their own hours
and they can live anywhere and do their work.
       "You could even live
       up here in these hills if you wanted."

              ✼

          Up North
        around Reedleaf Town
      there was this Ck'o'yo magician
     they called Kaup'a'ta or the Gambler.

          He was tall
       and he had a handsome face
  but he always wore spruce greens around his head, over his eyes.
    He dressed in the finest white buckskins
     his moccasins were perfectly sewn.

161

He had strings of sky blue turquoise
strings of red coral in his ears.
In all ways
the Gambler was very good to look at.

His house was high
in the peaks of the Zuni mountains
and he waited for people to wander
up to his place.
He kept the gambling sticks all stacked up
ready for them.

He walked and turned around
to show off his fancy clothes and expensive beads.
Then he told them he would gamble with them—
their clothes, their beads for his.
Most people wore their old clothes
when they went hunting in the mountains;
so they figured they didn't have much to lose.
Anyway, they might win all his fine things.
Not many could pass up his offer.

They ate the blue cornmeal
he offered them.
They didn't know
he mixed human blood with it.
Visitors who ate it
didn't have a chance.

He got power over them that way,
and when they started gambling with him
they did not stop until they lost
everything they owned.
And when they were naked
and he had everything
he'd say

"I tell you what.
Since I'm so good and generous
I'll give you one last chance.
See that rawhide bag hanging
on the north wall over there?
If you can guess what is in that bag
I'll give you back all your clothes and beads
and everything I have here too—
                these feather blankets
                all these strings of coral beads
                these fine white buckskin moccasins.
But if you don't guess right
you lose your life."

They were in his power.
They had lost everything.
It was their last chance.
So they usually said "okay"
but they never guessed
what was in the bag.

163

He hung them upside down in his storeroom,
side by side with the other victims.
He cut out their hearts
and let their blood run down
into the bins of blue cornmeal.

That is what the Ck'o'yo Kaup'a'ta did,
up there
in the Zuni mountains.
And one time
he even captured the stormclouds.
He won everything from them
but since they can't be killed,
all he could do
was lock them up
in four rooms of his house—
the clouds of the east in the east room
the clouds of the south in the south room
the clouds of the west in the west room
the clouds of the north in the north room.

The Sun is their father.
Every morning he wakes them up.
But one morning he went
first to the north top of the west mountain
then to the west top of the south mountain
and then to the south top of the east mountain;

164

and finally, it was on the east top of the north mountain
he realized they were gone.

For three years the stormclouds disappeared
while the Gambler held them prisoners.
The land was drying up
the people and animals were starving.

They are his children
so he went looking for them.
He took blue pollen and yellow pollen
he took tobacco and coral beads;
and he walked into the open country
below the mesas.
There, in a sandy place by a blue flower vine,
Spider Woman was waiting for him.

"Grandson," she said.
"I hear your voice," he answered
"but where are you?"
"Down here, by your feet."
He looked down at the ground and saw a little hole.

"I brought you something, Grandma."
"Why thank you, Grandson,
I can always use these things," she said.

"The stormclouds are missing."
"That Ck'o'yo Kaup'a'ta the Gambler has them locked up,"
she told him.
"How will I get them back?"

"It won't be easy, Grandson,
but here,
take this medicine.
Blow it on the Gambler's black ducks
who guard his place.
Take him by surprise.
The next thing is:
don't eat anything he offers you.
Go ahead
gamble with him.
Let him think he has you too.
Then he will make you his offer—
your life for a chance to win everything:
even his life.

He will say
"What do I have hanging in that leather bag
on my east wall?"
You say "Maybe some shiny pebbles,"
then you pause a while and say "Let me think."
Then guess again,
say "Maybe some mosquitoes."
He'll begin to rub his flint blade and say

166

"This is your last chance."
But this time you will guess
"The Pleiades!"
He'll jump up and say "Heheya'! You are the first to guess."
Next he will point to a woven cotton bag
hanging on the south wall.
He will say
"What is it I have in there?"
You'll say
"Could it be some bumblebees?"
He'll laugh and say "No!"
"Maybe some butterflies, the small yellow kind."
"Maybe some tiny black ants," you'll say.
"No!" Kaup'a'ta will be smiling then.
"This is it," he'll say.

But this is the last time, Grandson,
you say "Maybe you have Orion in there."
And then
everything—
his clothing, his beads, his heart
and the rainclouds
will be yours."

"Okay, Grandma, I'll go."
He took the medicine into the Zuni mountains.
He left the trail and walked high on one of the peaks.

167

The black ducks rushed at him
but he blew the medicine on them
before they could squawk.

He came up behind the Gambler
practicing with the sticks
on the floor of his house.

"I'm fasting," he told Kaup'a'ta,
when he offered him the blue cornmeal
"but thanks anyway."
Sun Man pulled out his things:
four sets of new clothes
two pairs of new moccasins
two strings of white shell beads
Kaup'a'ta smiled when he saw these things
"We'll gamble all night," he said.

It happened
just the way Spider Woman said:
When he had lost everything
Kaup'a'ta gave him a last chance.
The Gambler bet everything he had
that Sun Man couldn't guess what he had
in the bag on the east wall.
Kaup'a'ta was betting his life
that he couldn't guess
what was in the sack hanging from the south wall.

"Heheya'! You guessed right!
Take this black flint knife, Sun Man,
go ahead, cut out my heart, kill me."
Kaup'a'ta lay down on the floor
with his head toward the east.
But Sun Man knew Kaup'a'ta was magical
and he couldn't be killed anyway.
Kaup'a'ta was going to lie there
and pretend to be dead.

So Sun Man knew what to do:
He took the flint blade
and he cut out the Gambler's eyes
He threw them into the south sky
and they became the horizon stars of autumn.

Then he opened the doors of the four rooms
and he called to the stormclouds:
"My children," he said
I have found you!
Come on out. Come home again.
Your Mother, the Earth is crying for you.
Come home, children, come home."

❂

The purple asters are growing in wide fields around the red rocks past Mesita clear to the Sedillo Grant. This year there has been more rain here than I have ever seen. Yesterday at Dripping Springs I saw a blue flower I had never seen before, something like an orchid, growing from a succulent leafless bulb. So many of these plants had never bloomed in my lifetime and so I had assumed these plants did not bloom; now I find that through all these years they were only waiting for enough rain.

I remember the stories they used to tell us about places that were meadows full of flowers or about canyons that had wide clear streams. I remember our amazement at these stories of lush grass and running water because the places they spoke of had all changed; the places they spoke of were dry and covered with tumbleweeds and all that was left of the streams were deep arroyos. But I understand now. I will remember this September like they remembered the meadows and streams; I will talk about the yellow beeweed solid on all the hills, and maybe my grandchildren will also be amazed and wonder what has become of the fields of wild asters and all the little toads that sang in the evening. Maybe after they listen to me talking about this rainy lush September they will walk over the sandrock at the old house at Dripping Springs trying to imagine the pools of rainwater and the pollywogs of this year.

From a letter to Lawson F. Inada,
September 1975

❂

Simon J. Ortiz is a wonderful poet from McCartys (Acoma Pueblo) not far from Laguna. I owe a great deal to him for his encouragement when I was first beginning to write. Through the years we've had to depend a lot on the telephone and letters because whenever he was in New Mexico I was in Arizona or Alaska and whenever I was in New Mexico he was in California. "Uncle Tony's Goat" is from a story Simon told me when he called one morning about 4 A.M. and we had a long discussion about goats.

❂

170

We had a hard time finding the right kind of string to use. We knew we needed gut to string our bows the way the men did, but we were little kids and we didn't know how to get any. So Kenny went to his house and brought back a ball of white cotton string that his mother used to string red chili with. It was thick and soft and it didn't make very good bowstring. As soon as we got the bows made we sat down again on the sand bank above the stream and started skinning willow twigs for arrows. It was past noon, and the tall willows behind us made cool shade. There were lots of little minnows that day, flashing in the shallow water, swimming back and forth wildly like they weren't sure if they really wanted to go up or down the stream; it was a day for minnows that we were always hoping for— we could have filled our rusty coffee cans and old pickle jars full. But this was the first time for making bows and arrows, and the minnows weren't much different from the sand or the rocks now. The secret is the arrows. The ones we made were crooked, and when we shot them they didn't go straight—they flew around in arcs and curves; so we crawled through the leaves and branches, deep into the willow groves, looking for the best, the straightest willow branches. But even after we skinned the sticky wet bark from them and whittled the knobs off, they still weren't straight. Finally we went ahead and made notches at the end of each arrow to hook in the bowstring, and we started practicing, thinking maybe we could learn to shoot the crooked arrows straight.

We left the river each of us with a handful of damp, yellow arrows and our fresh-skinned willow bows. We walked slowly and shot arrows at bushes, big rocks, and the juniper tree that grows by Pino's sheep pen. They were working better just like we had figured; they still didn't fly straight, but now we could compensate for that by the way we aimed them. We were going up to the church to shoot at the cats old Sister Julian kept outside the cloister. We didn't want to hurt anything, just to have new kinds of things to shoot at.

But before we got to the church we went past the grassy hill where my uncle Tony's goats were grazing. A few of them were lying down chewing their cud peacefully, and they didn't seem to notice us. The billy goat was lying down, but he was watching us closely like he already knew about little kids. His yellow goat eyes didn't blink, and he stared with a wide, hostile look. The grazing goats made good deer for our bows. We shot all our arrows at the nanny goats and their kids; they skipped away from the careening arrows and never lost the rhythm of their greedy chewing as they continued to nibble the weeds and grass on the hillside. The billy goat was lying there watching us and taking us into his memory. As we ran down the road toward the church and Sister Julian's cats, I looked back, and my uncle Tony's billy goat was still watching me.

My uncle and my father were sitting on the bench outside the house when we walked by. It was September now, and the farming was almost over, except for bringing home the melons and a few pumpkins. They were mending ropes and bridles and feeling the afternoon sun. We held our bows and arrows out in front of us so they could see them. My father smiled and kept braiding the strips of leather in his hand, but my uncle Tony put down the bridle and pieces of scrap leather he was working on and looked at each of us kids slowly. He was old, getting some white hair—he was my mother's oldest brother, the one that scolded us when we told lies or broke things.

"You'd better not be shooting at things," he said, "only at rocks or trees. Something will get hurt. Maybe even one of you."

We all nodded in agreement and tried to hold the bows and arrows less conspicuously down at our sides; when he turned back to his work we hurried away before he took the bows away from us like he did the time we made the slingshot. He caught us shooting rocks at an old wrecked car; its windows were all busted out anyway, but he took the slingshot away. I always wondered what he did with it and with the knives we made ourselves out of tin cans. When I was much older I asked my mother, "What did he ever do with those knives and slingshots he took away from us?" She was kneading bread on the kitchen table at the time and was probably busy thinking about the fire in the oven outside. "I don't know," she said; "you ought to ask him yourself." But I never did. I thought about it lots of times, but I never did. It would have been like getting caught all over again.

The goats were valuable. We got milk and meat from them. My uncle was careful to see that all the goats were treated properly; the worst scolding my older sister ever got was when my mother caught her and some of her friends chasing the newborn kids. My mother kept saying over and over again, "It's a good thing I saw you; what if your uncle had seen you?" and even though we kids were very young then, we understood very well what she meant.

The billy goat never forgot the bows and arrows, even after the bows had cracked and split and the crooked, whittled arrows were all lost. This goat was big and black and important to my uncle Tony because he'd paid a lot to get him and because he wasn't an ordinary goat. Uncle Tony had bought him from a white man, and then he'd hauled him in the back of the pickup all the way from Quemado. And my uncle was the only person who could touch this goat. If a stranger or one of us kids got too near him, the mane on the billy goat's neck would stand on end and the goat would rear up on his hind legs and dance forward trying to reach the person with his long, spiral horns. This billy goat smelled bad, and none of us cared if we couldn't pet him. But my uncle took good care of this goat. The goat would let Uncle Tony brush him with the horse brush and scratch him around the base of his horns. Uncle Tony talked to the billy goat—in the morning when he unpenned the goats and in the evening when he gave them their hay and closed the gate for the night. I never paid too much attention to what he said to the billy goat;

usually it was something like "Get up, big goat! You've slept long enough," or "Move over, big goat, and let the others have something to eat." And I think Uncle Tony was proud of the way the billy goat mounted the nannies, powerful and erect with the great black testicles swinging in rhythm between his hind legs.

We all had chores to do around home. My sister helped out around the house mostly, and I was supposed to carry water from the hydrant and bring in kindling. I helped my father look after the horses and pigs, and Uncle Tony milked the goats and fed them. One morning near the end of September I was out feeding the pigs their table scraps and pig mash; I'd given the pigs their food, and I was watching them squeal and snap at each other as they crowded into the feed trough. Behind me I could hear the milk squirting into the eight-pound lard pail that Uncle Tony used for milking.

When he finished milking he noticed me standing there; he motioned toward the goats still inside the pen. "Run the rest of them out," he said as he untied the two milk goats and carried the milk to the house.

I was seven years old, and I understood that everyone, including my uncle, expected me to handle more chores; so I hurried over to the goat

173

pen and swung the tall wire gate open. The does and kids came prancing out. They trotted daintily past the pigpen and scattered out, intent on finding leaves and grass to eat. It wasn't until then I noticed that the billy goat hadn't come out of the little wooden shed inside the goat pen. I stood outside the pen and tried to look inside the wooden shelter, but it was still early and the morning sun left the inside of the shelter in deep shadow. I stood there for a while, hoping that he would come out by himself, but I realized that he'd recognized me and that he wouldn't come out. I understood right away what was happening and my fear of him was in my bowels and down my neck; I was shaking.

Finally my uncle came out of the house; it was time for breakfast. "What's wrong?" he called out from the door.

"The billy goat won't come out," I yelled back, hoping he would look disgusted and come do it himself.

"Get in there and get him out," he said as he went back into the house.

I looked around quickly for a stick or broom handle, or even a big rock, but I couldn't find anything. I walked into the pen slowly, concentrating on the darkness beyond the shed door; I circled to the back of the shed and kicked at the boards, hoping to make the billy goat run out. I put my eye up to a crack between the boards, and I could see he was standing up now and that his yellow eyes were on mine.

My mother was yelling at me to hurry up, and Uncle Tony was watching. I stepped around into the low doorway, and the goat charged toward me, feet first. I had dirt in my mouth and up my nose and there was blood running past my eye; my head ached. Uncle Tony carried me to the house; his face was stiff with anger, and I remembered what he'd always told us about animals; they won't bother you unless you bother them first. I didn't start to cry until my mother hugged me close and wiped my face with a damp wash rag. It was only a little cut above my eyebrow, and she sent me to school anyway with a Band-Aid on my forehead.

Uncle Tony locked the billy goat in the pen. He didn't say what he was going to do with the goat, but when he left with my father to haul firewood, he made sure the gate to the pen was wired tightly shut. He looked at the goat quietly and with sadness; he said something to the goat, but the yellow eyes stared past him.

"What's he going to do with the goat?" I asked my mother before I went to catch the school bus.

"He ought to get rid of it," she said. "We can't

have that goat knocking people down for no good reason."

I didn't feel good at school. The teacher sent me to the nurse's office and the nurse made me lie down. Whenever I closed my eyes I could see the goat and my uncle, and I felt a stiffness in my throat and chest. I got off the school bus slowly, so the other kids would go ahead without me. I walked slowly and wished I could be away from home for a while. I could go over to Grandma's house, but she would ask me if my mother knew where I was and I would have to say no, and she would make me go home first to ask. So I walked very slowly, because I didn't want to see the black goat's hide hanging over the corral fence.

When I got to the house I didn't see a goat hide or the goat, but Uncle Tony was on his horse and my mother was standing beside the horse holding a canteen and a flour sack bundle tied with brown string. I was frightened at what this meant. My uncle looked down at me from the saddle.

"The goat ran away," he said. "Jumped out of the pen somehow. I saw him just as he went over the hill beyond the river. He stopped at the top of the hill and he looked back this way."

Uncle Tony nodded at my mother and me and then he left; we watched his old roan gelding splash across the stream and labor up the steep path beyond the river. Then they were over the top of the hill and gone.

Uncle Tony was gone for three days. He came home early on the morning of the fourth day, before we had eaten breakfast or fed the animals. He was glad to be home, he said, because he was getting too old for such long rides. He called me over and looked closely at the cut above my eye. It had scabbed over good, and I wasn't wearing a Band-Aid any more; he examined it very carefully before he let me go. He stirred some sugar into his coffee.

"That goddamn goat," he said. "I followed him for three days. He was headed south, going straight to Quemado. I never could catch up to him." My uncle shook his head. "The first time I saw him he was already in the piñon forest, half-way into the mountains already. I could see him most of the time, off in the distance a mile or two. He would stop sometimes and look back." Uncle Tony paused and drank some more coffee. "I stopped at night. I had to. He stopped too, and in the morning we would start out again. The trail just gets higher and steeper. Yesterday morning there was frost on top of the blanket when I woke up and we were in the big pines and red oak leaves. I couldn't see him any more because the

175

forest is too thick. So I turned around." Tony finished the cup of coffee. "He's probably in Quemado by now."

I looked at him again, standing there by the door, ready to go milk the nanny goats.

"There wasn't ever a goat like that one," he said, "but if that's the way he's going to act, O.K. then. That damn goat got pissed off too easy anyway."

He smiled at me and his voice was strong and happy when he said this.

HOW TO WRITE A POEM ABOUT THE SKY

for the students of the Bethel Middle
School, Bethel, Alaska—Feb. 1975

You see the sky now
colder than the frozen river
so dense and white
little birds
walk across it.

You see the sky now
but the earth
is lost in it
and there are no horizons.
It is all
a single breath.

You see the sky
but the earth is called
by the same name
        the moment
        the wind shifts
sun splits it open
and bluish membranes
push through slits of skin.

You see the sky

IN COLD STORM LIGHT

In cold storm light
I watch the sandrock
   canyon rim.

   The wind is wet
      with the smell of piñon.
   The wind is cold
      with the sound of juniper.
         And then
           out of the thick ice sky
              running swiftly
              pounding
              swirling above the treetops
           The snow elk come,
         Moving, moving
             white song
             storm wind in the branches.
And when the elk have passed
    behind them
       a crystal train of snowflakes
       strands of mist
          tangled in rocks
         and leaves.

PRAYER TO THE PACIFIC

I traveled to the ocean
        distant
                from my southwest land of sandrock
                to the moving blue water
        Big as the myth of origin.

Pale
pale water in the yellow-white light of
                sun   floating west
                        to China
                where ocean herself was born.
Clouds that blow across the sand are wet.

Squat in the wet sand and speak to the Ocean:
            I return to you   turquoise   the red coral you sent us,
                    sister spirit of Earth.
Four round stones in my pocket   I carry back the ocean
                to suck and to taste.

Thirty thousand years ago
        Indians came riding across the ocean
        carried by giant sea turtles.

Waves were high that day
         great sea turtles waded   slowly out
                  from the gray sundown sea.
Grandfather Turtle rolled in the sand   four times
         and disappeared
               swimming into the sun.

And so   from that time
       immemorial,
            as the old people say,
rain clouds drift from the west
        gift from the ocean.

Green leaves in the wind
Wet earth on my feet
       swallowing raindrops
          clear from China.

HORSES AT VALLEY STORE

Everyday I meet the horses
   With dust and heat they come
      step by step
Pulling the day
  behind them.

At Valley Store
     there is water.
     Gray steel tank
     Narrow concrete trough.

Eyes that smell water,
In a line one by one
     moving with the weight of the sun
     moving through the deep earth heat
They come.

People with
  water barrels
  in pick-ups   in wagons
So they pause   and from their distance
     outside of time
They wait.

September 20, the day after Laguna Feast is my father's birthday. On that day, fifty-five years ago, Grandma Lillie said she worked all day at Abie's store; she even drove the old cut-down car to Seama to deliver groceries up there. Late that afternoon she finally went to bed and around six o'clock she heard the church bells ringing the Angelus. She was listening, she said, to the Angelus bells ringing and just as the bells finished ringing he was born.

❦❦

They found him under a big cottonwood tree. His Levi jacket and pants were faded light blue so that he had been easy to find. The big cottonwood tree stood apart from a small grove of winterbare cottonwoods which grew in the wide, sandy arroyo. He had been dead for a day or more, and the sheep had wandered and scattered up and down the arroyo. Leon and his brother-in-law, Ken, gathered the sheep and left them in the pen at the sheep camp before they returned to the cottonwood tree. Leon waited under the tree while Ken drove the truck through the deep sand to the edge of the arroyo. He squinted up at the sun and unzipped his jacket—it sure was hot for this time of year. But high and northwest the blue mountains were still in snow. Ken came sliding down the low, crumbling bank about fifty yards down, and he was bringing the red blanket.

Before they wrapped the old man, Leon took a piece of string out of his pocket and tied a small gray feather in the old man's long white hair. Ken gave him the paint. Across the brown wrinkled forehead he drew a streak of white and along the high cheekbones he drew a strip of blue paint.

He paused and watched Ken throw pinches of corn meal and pollen into the wind that fluttered the small gray feather. Then Leon painted with yellow under the old man's broad nose, and finally, when he had painted green across the chin, he smiled.

"Send us rain clouds, Grandfather." They laid the bundle in the back of the pickup and covered it with a heavy tarp before they started back to the pueblo.

They turned off the highway onto the sandy pueblo road. Not long after they passed the store and post office they saw Father Paul's car coming toward them. When he recognized their faces he slowed his car and waved for them to stop. The young priest rolled down the car window.

"Did you find old Teofilo?" he asked loudly.

Leon stopped the truck. "Good morning, Father. We were just out to the sheep camp. Everything is O.K. now."

"Thank God for that. Teofilo is a very old man. You really shouldn't allow him to stay at the sheep camp alone."

"No, he won't do that any more now."

"Well, I'm glad you understand. I hope I'll be seeing you at Mass this week—we missed you last Sunday. See if you can get old Teofilo to come with you." The priest smiled and waved at them as they drove away.

Louise and Teresa were waiting. The table was set for lunch, and the coffee was boiling on the black iron stove. Leon looked at Louise and then at Teresa.

"We found him under a cottonwood tree in the big arroyo near sheep camp. I guess he sat down to rest in the shade and never got up again." Leon walked toward the old man's bed. The red plaid shawl had been shaken and spread carefully over the bed, and a new brown flannel shirt and pair of stiff new Levi's were arranged neatly beside the pillow. Louise held the screen door open while Leon and Ken carried in the red blanket. He looked small and shriveled, and after they dressed him in the new shirt and pants he seemed more shrunken.

It was noontime now because the church bells rang the Angelus. They ate the beans with hot bread, and nobody said anything until after Teresa poured the coffee.

Ken stood up and put on his jacket. "I'll see

about the gravediggers. Only the top layer of soil is frozen. I think it can be ready before dark."

Leon nodded his head and finished his coffee. After Ken had been gone for a while, the neighbors and clanspeople came quietly to embrace Teofilo's family and to leave food on the table because the gravediggers would come to eat when they were finished.

The sky in the west was full of pale yellow light. Louise stood outside with her hands in the pockets of Leon's green army jacket that was too big for her. The funeral was over, and the old men had taken their candles and medicine bags and were gone. She waited until the body was laid into the pickup before she said anything to Leon. She touched his arm, and he noticed that her hands were still dusty from the corn meal that she had sprinkled around the old man. When she spoke, Leon could not hear her.

"What did you say? I didn't hear you."

"I said that I had been thinking about something."

"About what?"

"About the priest sprinkling holy water for Grandpa. So he won't be thirsty."

Leon stared at the new moccasins that Teofilo had made for the ceremonial dances in the summer. They were nearly hidden by the red blanket. It was getting colder, and the wind pushed gray dust down the narrow pueblo road. The sun was approaching the long mesa where it disappeared during the winter. Louise stood there shivering and watching his face. Then he zipped up his jacket and opened the truck door. "I'll see if he's there."

Ken stopped the pickup at the church, and Leon got out; and then Ken drove down the hill to the graveyard where people were waiting. Leon knocked at the old carved door with its symbols of the Lamb. While he waited he looked up at the twin bells from the king of Spain with the last sunlight pouring around them in their tower.

The priest opened the door and smiled when he saw who it was. "Come in! What brings you here this evening?"

The priest walked toward the kitchen, and Leon stood with his cap in his hand, playing with the earflaps and examining the living room—the brown sofa, the green armchair, and the brass lamp that hung down from the ceiling by links of chain. The priest dragged a chair out of the kitchen and offered it to Leon.

"No thank you, Father. I only came to ask you if you would bring your holy water to the graveyard."

The priest turned away from Leon and looked out the window at the patio full of shadows and the dining-room windows of the nuns' cloister across the patio. The curtains were heavy, and the light from within faintly penetrated; it was impossible to see the nuns inside eating supper. "Why didn't you tell me he was dead? I could have brought the Last Rites anyway."

Leon smiled. "It wasn't necessary, Father."

The priest stared down at his scuffed brown loafers and the worn hem of his cassock. "For a Christian burial it was necessary."

His voice was distant, and Leon thought that his blue eyes looked tired.

"It's O.K. Father, we just want him to have plenty of water."

The priest sank down into the green chair and picked up a glossy missionary magazine. He turned the colored pages full of lepers and pagans without looking at them.

"You know I can't do that, Leon. There should have been the Last Rites and a funeral Mass at the very least."

Leon put on his green cap and pulled the flaps down over his ears. "It's getting late, Father. I've got to go."

When Leon opened the door Father Paul stood up and said, "Wait." He left the room and came back wearing a long brown overcoat. He followed Leon out the door and across the dim churchyard to the adobe steps in front of the church. They both stooped to fit through the low adobe entrance. And when they started down the hill to the graveyard only half of the sun was visible above the mesa.

The priest approached the grave slowly, wondering how they had managed to dig into the frozen ground; and then he remembered that this was New Mexico, and saw the pile of cold loose sand beside the hole. The people stood close to each other with little clouds of steam puffing from their faces. The priest looked at them and saw a pile of jackets, gloves, and scarves in the yellow, dry tumbleweeds that grew in the graveyard. He looked at the red blanket, not sure that Teofilo was so small, wondering if it wasn't some perverse Indian trick—something they did in March to ensure a good harvest—wondering if maybe old Teofilo was actually at sheep camp

185

corraling the sheep for the night. But there he was, facing into a cold dry wind and squinting at the last sunlight, ready to bury a red wool blanket while the faces of his parishioners were in shadow with the last warmth of the sun on their backs.

His fingers were stiff, and it took him a long time to twist the lid off the holy water. Drops of water fell on the red blanket and soaked into dark icy spots. He sprinkled the grave and the water disappeared almost before it touched the dim, cold sand; it reminded him of something— he tried to remember what it was, because he thought if he could remember he might understand this. He sprinkled more water; he shook the container until it was empty, and the water fell through the light from sundown like August rain that fell while the sun was still shining, almost evaporating before it touched the wilted squash flowers.

The wind pulled at the priest's brown Franciscan robe and swirled away the corn meal and pollen that had been sprinkled on the blanket. They lowered the bundle into the ground, and they didn't bother to untie the stiff pieces of new rope that were tied around the ends of the blanket. The sun was gone, and over on the highway the eastbound lane was full of headlights. The priest walked away slowly. Leon watched him climb the hill, and when he had disappeared within the tall, thick walls, Leon turned to look up at the high blue mountains in the deep snow that reflected a faint red light from the west. He felt good because it was finished, and he was happy about the sprinkling of the holy water; now the old man could send them big thunderclouds for sure.

19

Many of the Navajo people would come back to the same houses year after year for Laguna Feast until finally they were good friends with the Laguna families and they would bring nice gifts when they came. Grandpa Hank had a friend like that, an old man from Alamo. Every year they were so glad to see each other, and the Navajo man would bring Grandpa something in the gunny sack he carried—sometimes little apricots the old man grew or a mutton shoulder. Grandpa would walk around the store and gather up things for his friend—coffee and sugar and a new pair of Levi's—things like that. I remember the last time the old Navajo man came looking for my grandpa. He came into the store and looked for Grandpa where Grandpa always stood, behind his desk in the corner. When he didn't see him, the old man asked for him and then we told him, "Henry passed away last winter." The old Navajo man cried, and then he left. He never came back anymore after that.

⧉

DEER DANCE/FOR YOUR RETURN

for Denny

If this
will hasten your return
then I will hold myself above you all night
blowing softly
down-feathered clouds
that drift above the spruce
and hide your eyes
as you are born back
to the mountain.

Years ago
through the yellow oak leaves
antlers polished like stones
in the canyon stream-crossing
    Morning turned in the sky
    when I saw you
    and I wanted the gift
    you carry on moon-color shoulders
    so big
    the size of you
    holds the long winter.

You have come home with me before
a long way down the mountain

The people welcome you.

I took
the best red blanket for you
the turquoise   the silver rings
were very old
                something familiar for you
                blue corn meal saved special.

While others are sleeping
I tie feathers on antlers
whisper close to you
                we have missed you
                I have longed for you.

Losses are certain
in the pattern of this dance
Over the terrain a hunter travels
blind curves in the trail
seize the breath
until it leaps away
loose again
to run the hills.
                Go quickly.

How beautiful
this last time
I touch you
                to believe
                and hasten the return

                    of lava-slope hills and
                    your next-year heart
Mine still beats
in the tall grass
where you stopped.
                        Go quickly.

Year by year
after the first snowfall
I will walk these hills and
        pray you will come again
I will go with a heart full for you
        to wait your return.

The neck pulse slacks,
then smoothes.
It has been a long time
Sundown forms change
Faces are unfamiliar
        As the last warmth goes
        from under my hand
        Hooves scatter rocks
        down the hillside
        and I turn to you
The run
for the length of the mountain
is only beginning.

❇

In the fall, the Laguna hunters go to the hills and mountains around Laguna Pueblo to bring back the deer. The people think of the deer as coming to give themselves to the hunters so that the people will have meat through the winter. Late in the winter the Deer Dance is performed to honor and pay thanks to the deer spirits who've come home with the hunters that year. Only when this has been properly done will the spirits be able to return to the mountain and be reborn into more deer who will, remembering the reverence and appreciation of the people, once more come home with the hunters.

❇

Grandpa graduated from Sherman Institute, an Indian School located in Riverside, California. While he was at Sherman he became fascinated with engineering and design and wanted to become an automobile designer. But in 1912 Indian schools were strictly vocational schools and the teachers at Sherman told Grandpa that Indians didn't become automobile designers. So when Grandpa Hank came home from Sherman he had been trained to be a store clerk.

He went to work in Abie Abraham's store at Laguna and eventually saved up enough to open a little store of his own after he and Grandma Lillie were married. He never cared much for storekeeping; he just did what had to be done. When I got older I was aware of how quiet he was sometimes and sensed there was some sadness he never identified.

He subscribed to *Motor Trend* and *Popular Mechanics* and followed the new car designs and results of road tests each year. In 1957 when Ford brought out the Thunderbird in a hardtop convertible, Grandpa Hank bought one and that was his car until he died.

A HUNTING STORY

for my grandpa, H. C. Marmon

You have
my grandfather's feet
light brown
smooth with the years
he's been gone.

Your hands are familiar
like the moonlight
on December snow
only sometimes,
I don't recognize
the sandstone cliff
behind you.

All night
your eyes
something burns dark
in old juniper trees.
the she-owl
echoes
along the cliff.
The stars
pull the sky down with them.

I smooth your belly
with my hand
round and round
We whisper
precise wet sand
spreading wide
down the Pacific Coast.

I knelt above you
that morning
I counted the rattles
the last whistles
in your throat.
I put my mouth on yours.

It might have been possible then
except you clenched your teeth
I could not push through
with my breath or my fingers.

I saw how you would go
spilling out
between ivory ribs
seeping under the tall gate
where earth sucked you in
like rainwater.

I couldn't stop you—
fragile dust
sparks of sunlight
dispersing
            into

horses of many colors
stony gray
blue steeldust
pink mesa stone
the yellow buckskin
leaping out of the east—
You scattered in all directions
of the winds.

Your wife and sons
burned your jacket
sold your car
They stood
holding their own fingers.

There was a song
you never sang to me
the same way
you'd never been to Zuni
not in all those years
of Arkansas, Santa Fe and Colorado.

There was a dance
sweetheart
you never came
to take me home
But when I hold fingers
they will be yours.

If I could see you clearly
only once
If I could come upon you
parked in your truck
sleeping in juniper trees
by Otter lake
Then we could gather
fluttering darkfeathered dreams
before they startle
before they fly far away.

The big star is Polaris
and we hunt for you.
Around smoky campfires
of First Night
where Navajo women
feed you mutton
and tell you
you are from the mountains
above Fluted Rock.

196

All night
I track sudden sounds
that crack
through moonlight thickets.

Up ahead
there is a small clearing
When you step out
into sight
I will be waiting.

❧

Grandpa Hank had grown up mostly at Paguate
with his Grandma and Grandpa Anaya
although his parents
lived at Laguna.
He used to drive an old wagon between Laguna and Paguate
and he used to pretend it was a fancy buggy
one of those light fast buggies.
Later on my great-grandpa bought a buggy
and it was Grandpa Hank's job
to drive tourists around the Laguna-Acoma area.
Grandpa Hank said
mostly the tourists came to see Acoma
the "Sky City" which was already famous then.

197

In 1908 when the Smithsonian Institution
excavated the top of *Katsi'ma,* Enchanted Mesa
Grandpa drove some of the archeologists
out there in his buggy.
The archeologists used a small brass cannon
to shoot a line over the top of Enchanted Mesa
so they could rig a crude elevator.
I asked Grandpa
what the archeologists found up there—
I had always been curious about what might be
on top of Enchanted Mesa.
"Did they find the bones of that old blind lady
and that baby," I asked him
"You know, the ones they tell about in that old story?"
There is an old story about a blind woman
being stranded on top of enchanted mesa with a tiny baby
the time the sandstone trail to the top collapsed.

"I didn't see any bones,"
                              Grandpa Hank said,
but those Smithsonian people were putting everything
into wooden boxes as fast as they could.
They took everything with them
in those wooden boxes
back to Washington D.C."
Then Grandpa said
                    "You know
                            probably all those boxes of things

they took from Enchanted Mesa
are still just sitting somewhere
in the basement of some museum."

WHERE MOUNTAIN LION LAY DOWN WITH DEER

I climb the black rock mountain
　stepping from day to day
　　　　　　　silently.
I smell the wind for my ancestors
　　pale blue leaves
　　crushed wild mountain smell.
Returning
　up the gray stone cliff
　where I descended
　　　　　　　a thousand years ago
Returning to faded black stone
where mountain lion lay down with deer.
It is better to stay up here
　　　　　　　watching wind's reflection
　　　　　　　in tall yellow flowers.
The old ones who remember me are gone
　　　　the old songs are all forgotten
and the story of my birth.

How I danced in snow-frost moonlight
     distant stars to the end of the Earth,
How I swam away
       in freezing mountain water
       narrow mossy canyon tumbling down
           out of the mountain
           out of deep canyon stone
      down
        the memory
             spilling out
             into the world.

DEER SONG

Storm winds carry snow
to the mountain stream
clotted white in silence,
pale blue streak under ice
to the sea.

The ice shatters into glassy
bone splinters that tear deep into
soft parts of the hoof.
Swimming away from the wolves
before dawn

choking back salt water
the steaming red froth tide.

It is necessary.
Reflections that blind
from a thousand feet of
gray schist
        snow-covered in dying winter sunlight.
The pain is numbed by the freezing,
        the depths of the night sky,
        the distance beyond pale stars.

Do not think that I do not love you
if I scream
        while I die.
Antler and thin black hoof
smashed against dark rock—
        the struggle is the ritual
shining teeth tangled in
        sinew and flesh.

You see,
        I will go with you,
Because you call softly
because you are my brother
        and my sister

Because the mountain is
our mother.
I will go with you
because you love me
while I die.

❁

At Laguna Feast time, Navajos used to jam the
hillsides with their wagons and horses. As a child
I watched them arrive. They braided red and
blue and yellow yarn tassles into the horses'
manes and tails, and they decorated their wagons. They came because years ago the Lagunas
invited them to come and eat all they wanted at
any house. After four or five days they'd go,
loaded with gifts from Laguna—corn, melons,
squash. Gradually, the wagons were fewer and
fewer, replaced by old beat-up cars and trucks.
My father made all of us kids come outside and
watch the last wagon come. It came two years by
itself and then no more.

❁

PREPARATIONS

Dead sheep
   beside the highway.
Belly burst open
     guts and life unwinding on the sand.

The body is carefully attended.
Look at the long black wings
      the shining eyes
Solemn and fat the crows gather
     to make preparations.

  Pull wool from skin
  Pick meat from bone
     tendon from muscle.
Only a few more days
   they say to each other
A few more days and this will be finished.

  Bones, bones
  Let wind polish the bones.
  It is done.

STORY FROM BEAR COUNTRY

You will know
when you walk
in bear country
By the silence
flowing swiftly between the juniper trees
by the sundown colors of sandrock
all around you.

You may smell damp earth
scratched away
from yucca roots
You may hear snorts and growls
slow and massive sounds
from caves
in the cliffs high above you.

It is difficult to explain
how they call you
All but a few who went to them
left behind families
            grandparents
            and sons
            a good life.

The problem is
you will never want to return

Their beauty will overcome your memory
like winter sun
melting ice shadows from snow
And you will remain with them
locked forever inside yourself
               your eyes will see you
               dark shaggy and thick.

We can send bear priests
loping after you
their medicine bags
bouncing against their chests
Naked legs painted black
bear claw necklaces
rattling against
their capes of blue spruce.

They will follow your trail
into the narrow canyon
through the blue-gray mountain sage
to the clearing
where you stopped to look back
and saw only bear tracks
behind you.

When they call
faint memories

will writhe around your heart
and startle you with their distance.
But the others will listen
because bear priests sing
beautiful songs
They must
if they are ever to call you back.

They will try to bring you
step by step
back to the place you stopped
and found only bear prints in the sand
where your feet had been.

Whose voice is this?
You may wonder
hearing this story when
after all
you are alone
hiking in these canyons and hills
while your wife and sons are waiting
back at the car for you.

But you have been listening to me
for some time now
from the very beginning in fact
and you are alone in this canyon of stillness
206 not even cedar birds flutter.

See, the sun is going down now
the sandrock is washed in its colors
Don't be afraid
>we love you
>we've been calling you
>all this time
Go ahead
turn around
see the shape
of your footprints
in the sand.

❧

He was a small child
learning to get around
by himself.
His family went by wagon
into the mountains near
Fluted Rock.

It was Fall and
they were picking piñons.
I guess he just wandered away
trying to follow his brothers and sisters
into the trees.

His aunt thought he was with his mother,
and she thought he was with his sister.

When they tracked him the next day
his tracks went into the canyon
near the place which belonged
to the bears. They went
as far as they could
to the place
where no human
could go beyond,
and his little footprints
were mixed in with bear tracks.

So they sent word for this medicine man
to come. He knew how
to call the child back again.

There wasn't much time.
The medicine man was running, and his
assistants followed behind him.

They all wore bearweed
tied at their wrists and ankles
and around their necks.

He grunted loudly and scratched on the ground in front of him
he kept watching the entrance of the bear cave.

He grunted and made a low growling sound.
Pretty soon the little bears came out
because he was making mother bear sounds.
He grunted and growled a little more
and then the child came out.
He was already walking like his sisters
he was already crawling on the ground.

They couldn't just grab the child.
They couldn't simply take him back
because he would be in–between forever
and probably he would die.

They had to call him.
Step by step the medicine man
brought the child back.

So, long time ago
they got him back again
but he wasn't quite the same
after that
not like the other children.

Grandma A'mooh used to tell me stories she remembered hearing when she was a girl. One time, she said, some Navajos came and ran off a big herd of Laguna sheep. The Laguna men all got together and went after them. The Navajos were headed north but they couldn't travel very fast because they were driving all those sheep ahead of them. So finally, a little way past Paguate toward Moquino, they caught up with the Navajos. But the Lagunas didn't harm them or take them captive. They just asked the Navajos why they had taken the sheep, and the Navajos said it was because they were very hungry and had nothing to eat. So the Lagunas told them that next time they needed food to come ask for it instead of stealing it and the Laguna people would be happy to give them something. Then the Lagunas gave them five or six sheep and let them go. Grandma was always proud of this story because her uncles and grandfather had been there.

At Laguna Feast time, on September 19, Navajo people are welcome at any Laguna home regardless of whether they are acquainted or not. When Navajo people knock, they are invited in to eat as much as they want. And no matter how much they eat, they are never refused another helping of bread or chili stew.

Most of the scouts were at the corral catching their horses and saddling up. I saw them there, busy, getting ready to go; and the feeling of excitement hit me in the stomach. I walked faster. The dust in the first corral was so thick I couldn't see clearly. The horses were running in crowded circles while the men tried to rope them. Whenever someone threw a rope, all the horses would bolt away from it, carrying their heads low. I didn't see our horses. Maybe Mariano thought that me and my uncle weren't going and he left our horses in the pasture.

For a while it had looked like my uncle couldn't go this time because of his foot: he tripped over a big rock one night when he was coming back from the toilet and broke some little bones in his foot. The "sparrow bones" he called them, and he wrapped up his foot in a wide piece of buckskin and wore his moccasins instead of cavalry boots. But when Captain Pratt came to the house the night after they got the message about Geronimo, Siteye shook his head.

"Shit," he said, "these Lagunas can't track Geronimo without me."

Captain said, "O.K."

Siteye sat there staring out the screen door into the early evening light; then he looked at me. "I think I'll bring my nephew along. To saddle my horse for me."

Captain nodded.

The other corral was full of horses: they were standing quietly because nobody was in there trying to catch them. They saw me coming and backed away from me, snorting and crowding each other into the corner of the corral. I saw Rainbow right away. My uncle's horse. A tall, strong horse that my uncle bought from a Mexican at Cubero; my uncle has to have a big horse to carry him. The horses that we raise at Laguna don't get as powerful as Rainbow; but they eat less. Rainbow always ate twice as much. Like my uncle, Siteye is a big man—tall and really big—not fat though, big like an elk who is fast and strong—big like that. I got the lariat rope ready and stepped inside the corral; the horses crowded themselves into the corners and watched me, probably trying to figure out which one of them I was going to catch. Rainbow was easy to catch; he can't duck his head down as low as the others. He was fat and looked good. I put the bridle on him and led him out the gate, watching, careful to see that one of the others didn't try to sneak out the gate behind us. It was hard to swing the saddle onto his back; Siteye's saddle is a heavy Mexican saddle—I still use it, and even now it seems heavy to me.

The cinch would hardly reach around his belly. "Goddamn it, horse," I told him, "don't swell up your belly for me." I led him around a little to fool him, so he would let the air out, then I tightened the cinch some more. He sighed like horses do when you cinch them up good and they know you've got them. Then, when I was finished, all I had to do was drop the bridle reins, because this horse was specially trained to stand like he was tied up whenever you drop the reins in front of him, and he would never wander away, even to eat. I petted him on the neck before I went to catch my horse. Rainbow was such a beautiful color too—dark brown with long streaks of white on each of his sides—streaks that ran from behind his ears to the edge of his fat flanks. He looked at me with gentle eyes. That's a funny thing about horses—wild and crazy when they are loose in corral together, and so tame when they've got a saddle on them.

My horse was a little horse; he wasn't tall or stout—he was like the old-time Indian horses— that's what my father told me. The kind of horse that can run all day long and not get tired or have to eat much. Best of all he was gold-colored—a dark red-gold color with a white mane and tail. The Navajos had asked twenty dollars for him when they were only asking twelve dollars for their other saddle horses. They wanted cash—gold or silver—no trade. But my mother had a sewing machine—one that some white lady had given her. My mother said it sewed too fast for her, almost ran over her fingers. So we offered them this new sewing machine with silver engraved trimming and a wooden case. They took the sewing machine, and that's how I got my first horse. That day he was hard to catch. He could hide in between the bigger horses and escape my rope. By the time I managed to catch him I could hear Siteye yelling at me from the other corral.

"Andy!" he called, "Andy, where's my horse? We're ready to go."

It was almost noon when we crossed the river below the pueblo and headed southwest. Captain Pratt was up ahead, and Siteye and Sousea were riding beside him. I stayed behind, because I didn't want to get in anyone's way or do anything wrong. We were moving at a steady fast walk. It was late April, and it wasn't too cold or too hot—a good time of year when you can travel all day without any trouble. Siteye stayed up ahead for a long time with Captain, but finally he dropped back to ride with me for a while; maybe he saw that I was riding all by myself. He didn't speak for a long time. We were riding past Crow Mesa when he finally said something.

"We'll stop to eat pretty soon."

"Good," I said, "because I'm hungry." I looked at Siteye. His long, thick hair was beginning to turn white; his thighs weren't as big as they once had been, but he's still strong, I said to myself, he's not old.

"Where are we going?" I asked him again, to make sure.

"Pie Town, north of Datil. Captain says someone there saw Apaches or something."

We rode for a while in silence.

"But I don't think Geronimo is there. He's still at White Mountain."

"Did you tell Captain?"

"I told him, and he agrees with me. Geronimo isn't down there. So we're going down."

"But if you already know that Geronimo isn't there," I said, "why do you go down there to look for him?" He just looked at me and smiled.

Siteye reached into his saddle pack and pulled out a sack full of gumdrops and licorice. He took two or three pieces of candy and handed me the bag. The paper sack rattled when I reached into

it, and my horse shied away from the noise. I lost my balance and would have fallen off, but Siteye saw and he grabbed my left arm to steady me. I dismounted to pick up the bag of candy; only a few pieces had spilled when it fell. I put them in my mouth and held the quivering horse with one hand and rattled the paper bag with the other. After a while he got used to the sound and quit jumping.

"He better quit that," I said to Siteye after we started again. "He can't jump every time you give me a piece of candy."

Siteye shook his head. "Navajo horses. Always shy away from things." He paused. "It will be a beautiful journey for you. The mountains and the rivers. You've never seen them before."

"Maybe next time I come we'll find Geronimo," I said.

"Umm." That's all Siteye said. Just sort of grunted like he didn't agree with me but didn't want to talk about it either.

We stopped below Owl's Rock to eat; Captain had some of the scouts gather wood for a fire, and he pulled a little tin pot out of his big leather saddlebag. He always had tea, Siteye said. No matter where they were or what kind of weather. Siteye handed me a piece of dried deer meat; he motioned with his chin toward Captain.

"See that," he said to me, "I admire him for that. Not like a white man at all; he has plenty of time for some tea."

It was a few years later that I heard how some white people felt about Captain drinking Indian tea and being married to a Laguna woman. "Squaw man." But back then I wondered what Siteye was talking about.

"Only one time when he couldn't have tea for lunch. When Geronimo or some Apache hit that little white settlement near the Mexican border." Siteye paused and reached for the army-issue canteen by my feet. "That was as close as the Apaches ever got. But by the time we got there the people had been dead at least three days. The Apaches were long gone, as people sometimes say."

It was beautiful to hear Siteye talk; his words were careful and thoughtful, but they followed each other smoothly to tell a good story. He would pause to let you get a feeling for the words; and even silence was alive in his stories.

"Wiped out—all of them. Women and children. Left them laying all over the place like sheep when coyotes are finished with them." He paused for a long time and carefully rewrapped the jerky in the cheesecloth and replaced it in the saddle pouch. Then he rolled himself a cigarette and licked the wheat paper slowly, using his lips and tongue.

"It smelled bad. That was the worst of it—the smell."

"What was it like?" I asked him.

"Worse than a dead dog in August," he said, "an oily smell that stuck to you like skunk odor. They even left a dead man in the well so I had to ride back four miles to Salado Creek to take a bath and wash my clothes." He lit the cigarette he'd just rolled and took a little puff into his mouth. "The Ninth Cavalry was there. They wanted Captain to take us scouts and get going right away."

Siteye offered me the Bull Durham pouch and the wheat papers. I took them and started making a cigarette; he watched me closely.

"Too much tobacco," he said, "no wonder yours look like tamales."

I lit the cigarette and Siteye continued.

"The smell was terrible. I went over to Captain and I said, 'Goddamn it, Captain, I have to take a bath. This smell is on me.' He was riding around with his handkerchief over his mouth and nose so he couldn't talk—he just nodded his head.

215

Maybe he wanted to come with us, but he had to stay behind with the other officers who were watching their men dig graves. One of the officers saw us riding away and he yelled at us, but we just kept going because we don't have to listen to white men." There was a silence like Siteye had stopped to think about it again. "When we got back one of the officers came over to me; he was angry. 'Why did you go?' he yelled at me. I said to him, 'That dirty smell was all over us. It was so bad we knew the coyotes would come down from the hills tonight to carry us away—mistaking us for rotten meat.' The officer was very upset—maybe because I mentioned rotten meat, I don't know. Finally he rode away and joined the other officers. By then the dead were all buried and the smell was already fading away. We started on the trail after the Apaches, and it is a good thing that scouts ride up ahead because they all smelled pretty bad—especially the soldiers who touched the dead. 'Don't get down wind from the army.' That's what we said to each other the rest of the week while we hunted Geronimo."

We started to ride again. The sun had moved around past us, and in a few more hours it would be dark. Siteye rode up front to talk to the other scouts and smoke. I watched the country we were riding into: the rocky piñon foothills high above the Acoma mesas. The trail was steep now, and the trees and boulders were too close to the trail. If you didn't watch where you were going, the branches would slap your face. I had never been this far south before. This was Acoma land, and nobody from Laguna would come to hunt here unless he was invited.

The sun disappeared behind the great black mesa we were climbing, but below us, in the wide Acoma valley, the sunlight was bright and yellow on the sandrock mesas. We were riding into the shadows, and I could feel night approaching. We camped in the narrow pass that leads into the malpais country north of the Zuni Mountains.

"Hobble the horses, Andy. We're still close enough that they will try to go home tonight," Siteye told me. "All four feet."

I hobbled them, with each foot tied close to the other so that they could walk slowly or hop but couldn't run. The clearing we camped in had plenty of grass but no water. In the morning there would be water when we reached the springs at Moss-Covered Rock. The horses could make it until then. We ate dried meat and flaky-dry sheets of thin corn-batter bread; we all had tea with Captain. Afterward everyone sat near the fire, because winter still lingered on this high mesa where no green leaves or new grass had appeared. Siteye told me to dig a trench for us, and before we lay down, I buried hot coals under the dirt in the bottom of the trench. I rolled up in my blanket and could feel the warmth beneath me. I lay there and watched the stars for a long time. Siteye was singing a spring song to the stars; it was an old song with words about rivers and oceans in the sky. As I was falling asleep I remember the Milky Way—it was an icy snow river across the sky.

The lava flow stretches for miles north to south; and the distance from east to west is difficult to see. Small pines and piñons live in places where soil has settled on the black rock; in these places there are grasses and shrubs; rabbits and a few deer live there. It is a dark stone ocean with waves and ripples and deep holes. The Navajos believe that the lava is a great pool of blood from a dangerous giant whom the Twin Brothers killed a long time ago. We rode down the edge of the lava on a trail below the sandrock cliffs which rise above the lava; in some places there is barely room for two horses to pass side by side. The black rock holds the warmth of the sun, and the grass and leaves were turning green faster than the plants and bushes of the surrounding country.

When we stopped for lunch we were still traveling along the edge of the lava. I had never walked on it, and there is something about seeing it that makes you want to walk on it—to see how it feels under your feet and to walk in this strange place. I was careful to stay close to the edge, because I know it is easy to lose sight of landmarks and trails. Pretty soon Siteye came. He was walking very slowly and limping with his broken foot. He sat down on a rock beside me.

"Our ancestors have places here," he commented as he looked out over the miles of black rock. "In little caves they left pottery jars full of food and water. These were places to come when somebody was after you." He stood up and started back slowly. "I suppose the water is all gone now," he said, "but the corn might still be good."

When we finally left the lava flow behind us and moved into the foothills of the Zuni Moun-

217

tains, Siteye looked behind us over the miles of shining black rock. "Yes," he said, "it's a pretty good place. I don't think Geronimo would even travel out there."

Siteye had to ride up front most of the time after we entered the Zuni Mountains. Captain didn't know the trail, and Sousea wasn't too sure of it. Siteye told me later on he wasn't sure either, but he knew how to figure it out. That night we camped in the high mountains, where the pines are thick and tall. I lay down in my blanket and watched the sky fill with heavy clouds; and later in the night, rain came. It was a light, spring rain that came on the mountain wind. At dawn the rain was gone, and I still felt dry in my blanket. Before we left, Siteye and Captain squatted in the wet mountain dirt, and Siteye drew maps near their feet. He used his forefinger to draw mountains and canyons and trees.

Later on, Siteye told me, "I've only been this way once before. When I was a boy. Younger than you. But in my head, when I close my eyes, I can still see the trees and the boulders and the way the trail goes. Sometimes I don't remember the distance—things are closer or farther than I had remembered them, but the direction is right."

I understood him. Since I was a child my father had taught me, and Siteye had taught me, to remember the way: to remember how the trees look—dead branches or crooked limbs; to look for big rocks and to remember their shape and their color; and if there aren't big rocks, then little ones with pale-green lichens growing on them. To know the trees and rocks all together with the mountains and sky and wildflowers. I closed my eyes and tested my vision of the trail we had traveled so far. I could see the way in my head, and I had a feeling for it too—a feeling for how far the great fallen oak was from Mossy Rock springs.

"Once I couldn't find the trail off Big Bead Mesa. It was getting dark. I knew the place was somewhere nearby; then I saw an old gray snake crawling along a sandy wash. His rattles were yellowy brown and chipped off like an old man's toenails." Siteye rearranged his black felt hat and cleared his throat. "I remembered him. He lived in a hole under a twisted tree at the top of the trail. The night was getting chilly, because it was late September. So I figured that he was probably going back to his hole to sleep. I followed him. I was careful not to get too close—that would have offended him, and he might have gotten angry and gone somewhere else just to keep me away from his hole. He took me to the trail."

Siteye laughed. "I was just a little kid then, and I was afraid of the dark. I ran all the way down the trail, and I didn't stop until I got to my house."

By sundown we reached Pie Town. It didn't look like Geronimo had been there. The corrals were full of cows and sheep; no buildings had been burned. The windmill was turning slowly, catching golden reflections of the sun on the spinning wheel. Siteye rode up front with Sousea and Captain. They were looking for the army that was supposed to meet us here. I didn't see any army horses, but then I didn't see any horses at all. Then a soldier came out of the two-story house; he greeted Captain and they talked. The soldier pointed toward the big arroyo behind the town.

Captain told us that they were keeping all the horses in a big corral in the arroyo because they expected Geronimo any time. We laughed while we rode down the sloping path into the wide arroyo. Siteye handed me Captain's sorrel mare and Rainbow for me to unsaddle and feed. I filled three gunny-sack feedbags with crushed corn that I found in the barn. I watched them eat: tossing their heads up in the air and shaking the bags to reach the corn. They stood still when it was all gone, and I pulled the feedbags off over their ears. I took the feedbags off the other Laguna horses, then I tossed them all a big pile of hay. In the other half of the corral the Pie Town horses and army mounts had gathered to watch the Laguna horses eat. They watched quietly. It was dark by the time I finished with the horses, and everyone else had already gone up to the big house to eat. The shadows in the arroyo were black and deep. I walked slowly, and I heard a mourning dove calling from the tamarack trees.

They would have good food, I knew that. This place was named for the good pies that one of the women could make. I knocked on the screen door, and inside I could see an old white woman in a red checkered dress; she walked with a limp. She opened the door and pointed toward the kitchen. The scouts were eating in there, except for Captain who was invited to eat with the white people in the dining room. I took a big plate from the end of the table and filled it up with roast meat and beans; on the table there were two plates of hot, fresh bread. There was plenty of coffee, but I didn't see any pies. Siteye finished and pushed his plate aside; he poured himself another cup of coffee.

"Looks like all the white people in this area

moved up here from Quemado and Datil. In case Geronimo comes. All crowded together to make their last stand." Siteye laughed at his own joke. "It was some Major Littlecock who sent out the Apache alert. He says he found an Apache camp-site near here. He wants us to lead him to Geronimo." Siteye shook his head. "We aren't hunting deer," he said, "we're hunting people. With deer I can say, 'Well, I guess I'll go to Pie Town and hunt deer,' and I can probably find some around here. But with people you must say, 'I want to find these people—I wonder where they might be.'"

Captain came in. He smiled. "We tried to tell him. Both of us."

Siteye nodded his head. "Captain even had me talk to him, and I told him in good English, I said, 'Major, it is so simple. Geronimo isn't even here. He's at White Mountain. They are still hunting meat,' I told him. 'Meat to dry and carry with them this spring.'"

Captain was sitting in the chair besides me. He brought out his tobacco and passed it around the table. We all rolled ourselves a cigarette. For a while nobody said anything; we all sat there smoking and resting our dinner.

Finally Mariano said, "Hey, where are we going to sleep tonight? How about this kitchen?"

"You might eat everything," Siteye answered.

"I think it will be O.K. to sleep in the kitchen," Captain said.

Then Major Littlecock came in. We all stared, and none of us stood up for him; Laguna scouts never did that for anyone. Captain didn't stand up, because he wasn't really in the army either—only some kind of civilian volunteer that they hired because once he had been in their army. Littlecock wasn't young; he was past thirty and his hair was falling out. He was short and pale, and he kept rubbing his fingertips together.

He spoke rapidly. "I will show you the Apache camp in the morning. Then I want you to track them down and send a scout back to lead me to the place. We'll be waiting here on alert." He paused and kept his eyes on the wall above our heads. "I can understand your error concerning Geronimo's location. But we have sophisticated communications—so I couldn't expect you to be aware of Geronimo's movements."

He smiled nervously, then with great effort he examined us. We were wearing our Indian clothes —white cotton pants, calico shirts, and woven Hopi belts. Siteye had his black wide-brim hat, and most of us were wearing moccasins.

"Weren't you boys issued uniforms?" the Major asked.

Siteye answered him. "We wear them in the winter. It's too hot for wool now."

Littlecock looked at Captain. "Our Crow Indian boys preferred their uniforms," he said.

There was silence. It wasn't hostile, but nobody felt like saying anything—I mean, what was there to say? Crow Indian scouts like army uniforms, and Laguna scouts wear them only if it gets cold. Finally Littlecock moved toward the door to leave.

Captain stood up. "I was thinking the men could sleep here in the kitchen, Major. It would be more comfortable for them."

Littlecock's face was pale; he moved slowly. "I regret, Captain, that isn't possible. Army regulations on using civilian quarters—the women," he said, "you know what I mean. Of course, Captain, you're welcome to sleep here." Littlecock smiled, he was looking at all of us: "You boys won't mind sleeping with the horses, will you?"

Siteye looked intently at the Major's face and spoke to him in Laguna. "You are the one who has a desire for horses at night, Major, you sleep with them."

We all started laughing.

Littlecock looked confused. "What did he say, Captain Pratt? Could you translate that for me, please?" His face was red and he looked angry.

Captain was calm. "I'm sorry, Major, but I don't speak the Laguna language very well. I didn't catch the meaning of what Siteye said."

Littlecock knew he was lying. He faced Captain squarely and spoke in a cold voice. "It is very useful to speak the Indian languages fluently, Mr. Pratt. I have mastered Crow and Arapaho, and I was fluent in Sioux dialects before I was transferred here." He looked at Siteye, then he left the room.

We got up from the table. Siteye belched loudly and rearranged his hat. Mariano and George reached into the woodbox by the stove and made little toothpicks for themselves out of the kindling chips.

We walked down the arroyo, joking and laughing about sleeping out with the horses instead of inside where the white soldiers were sleeping.

"Remind me not to come back to this place," Mariano said.

"I only came because they pay me," George said, "and next time they won't even be able to pay me to come here."

Siteye cleared his throat. "I am only sorry that the Apaches aren't around here," he said. "I can't think of a better place to wipe out. If we see them tomorrow we'll tell them to come here first."

We were all laughing now, and we felt good

221

saying things like this. "Anybody can act violently—there is nothing to it; but not every person is able to destroy his enemy with words." That's what Siteye always told me, and I respect him.

We built a big fire to sit around. Captain came down later and put his little teapot in the hot coals; for a white man he could talk the Laguna language pretty good, and he liked to listen to the jokes and stories, though he never talked much himself. And Siteye told me once that Captain didn't like to brew his Indian tea around white people. "They don't approve of him being married to an Indian woman and they don't approve of Indian tea, either." Captain drank his tea slowly and kept his eyes on the flames of the fire. A long time after he had finished the tea he stood up slowly. "Sleep good," he said to us, and he rolled up in his big gray Navajo blanket. Siteye rolled himself another cigarette, while I covered the hot coals with sand and laid our blankets on top.

Before I went to sleep I said to Siteye, "You've been hunting Geronimo for a long time, haven't you? And he always gets away."

"Yes," Siteye said, staring up at the stars, "but I always like to think that it's us who get away."

At dawn the next day Major Littlecock took us to his Apache campsite. It was about four miles due west of Pie Town, in the pine forest. The cavalry approached the area with their rifles cocked, and the Major was holding his revolver. We followed them closely.

"Here it is." Littlecock pointed to a corral woven with cedar branches. There was a small hearth with stones around it; that was all.

Siteye and Sousea dismounted and walked around the place without stopping to examine the hearth and without once stopping to kneel down to look at the ground more closely. Siteye finally stopped outside the corral and rolled himself a cigarette; he made it slowly, tapping the wheat paper gently to get just the right distribution of tobacco. I don't think I ever saw him take so long to roll a cigarette. Littlecock had dismounted and was walking back and forth in front of his horse, waiting. Siteye lit the cigarette and took two puffs before he walked over to Captain. He shook his head.

"Some Mexican built himself a sheep camp here, Captain, that's all." Siteye looked at the Major to make certain he would hear. "No Geronimo here, like we said."

Pratt nodded his head.

Littlecock mounted; he had lost, and he knew it. "Accept my apology for this inconvenience,

Captain Pratt. I simply did not want to take any chances."

He looked at all of us; his face had a troubled, dissatisfied look; maybe he was wishing for the Sioux country up north, where the land and the people were familiar to him.

Siteye felt the same. If he hadn't killed them all, he could still be up there chasing Sioux; he might have been pretty good at it.

It was still early in the day; the forest smelled green and wet. I got off my horse to let him drink in the little stream. The water was splashing and shining in sunlight that fell through the treetops. I knelt on a mossy rock and felt the water. Cold water—a snow stream. I closed my eyes and I drank it. "Precious and rare," I said to myself, "water that I have not tasted, water that I may never taste again."

The rest of the scouts were standing in the shade discussing something. Siteye walked over to me.

"We'll hunt," he said. "Good deer country down here."

By noontime there were six bucks and a fat doe hanging in the trees near the stream. We ate fresh liver for lunch and afterwards I helped them bone out the meat into thin strips, and Sousea salted it and strung it on a cotton line; he hung it in the sun and started to dry it. We stayed all afternoon, sleeping and talking. Before the sun went down I helped Sousea put the pounds of salted meat strips into gunny sacks and tie them on the kitchen burros, who hardly had anything left to carry. When we got back to Pie Town it had been dark for a long time.

In the morning the white ladies made us a big meal; we took a long time to eat, and it was almost noon before we started northeast again. We went slowly and stopped early so Sousea could hang the meat out to dry for a few hours each day. When we got back to Flower Mountain I could see Laguna on the hill in the distance.

"Here we are again," I said to Siteye.

We stopped. Siteye turned around slowly and looked behind us at the way we had come: the canyons, the mountains, the rivers we had passed. We sat there for a long time remembering the way, the beauty of our journey. Then Siteye shook his head gently. "You know," he said, "that was a long way to go for deer hunting."

I just fed the rooster a blackened banana I found in the refrigerator. He has been losing his yellowish collar feathers lately, and I'm afraid it might be that he isn't getting enough to eat. But I suppose it could be his mean streak too—he is a rooster out of all the rooster stories my grandmother ever told me—the rooster who waited inside the barn on winter mornings when it was still dark and my grandma was just married and going to milk her father-in-law's cow. The rooster would wait and ambush her just when she thought she had escaped him. It was a reflexive reaction the morning he jumped to rake her with his spurs and she swung the milking bucket at him. He collapsed and didn't move, and the whole time she was milking the cow she wondered how she could ever tell her father-in-law, my great-grandfather, that she had killed his rooster. She took the milk inside and he was already up drinking his coffee. (He was an old man by then, the old white man who came from Ohio and married my great-grandmother from Pagu-ate village north of Laguna.) She told him she didn't mean to kill the rooster but that the bucket hit him too hard. They tell me that my great-grandfather was a very gentle person. And Grandma Lillie said that morning he told her not to worry, that he had known for a while that the rooster was too mean to keep. But as they went out to the barn together, to dispose of the dead rooster, there he was in the corral. Too mean to die, Grandma said. But after that, the rooster left her alone when she went out to milk the cow.

There are all kinds of other rooster stories that one is apt to hear. I am glad I have this rooster because I never quite believed roosters so consistently *were* like the stories tell us they are. On these hot Tucson days, he scratches a little nest in the damp dirt under the Mexican lime tree by the front door. It is imperative for him that the kittens and the black cat show him respect, even deference, by detouring or half-circling the rooster as they approach the water dish which is also under the lime tree. If they fail to do this, then he jumps up and stamps his feet moving sideways until they cringe. This done, he goes back to his mud nest.

He has all of us fooled, stepping around him softly, hesitant to turn our backs to him, all of us except for the old black hound dog. She won't let anyone, including the rooster, come between her and her food dish. The rooster pretends he does not notice her lack of concern; he pretends he was just finished eating when she approaches.

The lady at the feed store had to give him away. He was her pet and he let her pick him up and stroke him. But the men who came to buy hay got to teasing him and he started going after all the feed store customers. She was afraid he might hurt a child. So I took him and told her I didn't know how long he'd last here at the ranch because the coyotes are everywhere in the Tucson mountains. I didn't expect him to last even a week. But that was in June and now it is October. Maybe it is his meanness after all, that keeps the coyotes away, that makes his feathers fall out.

From a Letter to James A. Wright, Fall, 1978

But sometimes what we call "memory" and what we call "imagination" are not so easily distinguished.

I know Aunt Susuie and Aunt Alice would tell me stories they had told me before but with changes in details or descriptions. The story was the important thing and little changes here and there were really part of the story. There were even stories about the different versions of stories and how they imagined these differing versions came to be.

I've heard tellers begin "The way I heard it was. . . ." and then proceed with another story purportedly a version of a story just told but the story they would tell was a wholly separate story, a new story with an integrity of its own, an offspring, a part of the continuing which storytelling must be. Grandma Lillie was talking recently about years ago when she went out to milk my Great-grandpa Marmon's cow and the mean old rooster attacked her so she took a big rock and hit it and killed it. I told her that I thought I remembered her saying that the rooster was only stunned, not dead. "No," she said, "He jumped out of the dark with his claws right at me. Scared me so bad I picked up a big rock and hit him on the head and killed him. I was afraid to tell Grandpa Marmon, poor thing, he was such a nice old man." The coyotes finally got Rooster too. They'd been prowling near the house for a long time—it must have taken four of them—one to lure away the old black hound and the pup, and the other three to grab the chickens. There was almost no trace that the two little white hens had ever been at the ranch. I had to search a long time before I found even one white feather. But Rooster had put up a terrible fight and four piles of his dark green and black feathers were in front of the house. Coyotes waste nothing. There were no traces of blood, no remains at all, just the feathers. Later that afternoon the wind blew dust and a few drops of rain. The feathers scattered down the hillside catching in weeds under the creosote bushes and palo verde trees. There was nothing to bury; it was as if Rooster had just disappeared.

There have been other times when he disappeared and I searched everywhere for him—under the big jojoba bush he liked, on the screened porch and around by the windmill. One afternoon I even searched for him on horseback because I was certain he was nowhere near the house. Much later that day he simply reappeared. Last summer I was in the kitchen talking with Denny when suddenly I felt we were not alone—a strange feeling for the ranch which is miles from town. We checked the front door and the other rooms. Finally I went to the kitchen window. The rooster was standing motionless below the window screen listening to us. I saw by the fierceness of his little yellow eyes it was deliberate.

It's been weeks now, but this morning I went out and there was a single feather by the door. It is glossy and lies smooth; its colors are vivid—emerald green flecked with gold.

COYOTES AND THE STRO'RO'KA DANCERS

Long ago
near the Acoma mesa
there was another mesa
with very precipitous walls.
A lone coyote appeared
on the mesa top.
Down below in the valley
there was a group
of ceremonial dancers
the *Stro'ro'ka Ka'tsinas*
who were holding a dance.
And he was thrilled
with the sight
and he said
>"My! Look down below!
>Those dancers have beautiful costumes
>they have brought wonderful things
>to eat—
>>melons and squashes!"

Things that the Lagunas,
the Keres people,
have always had as food
from way back traditional
in the traditional state
>and
>>"How could one get
>>all that food?"

                    So he said
                "I think I'll call
                my clanspeople
                the Coyote Clan."
So he got to the very edge
and he gave this cry,
                this signal:
                        "Ama doo roo a roo!"
                        Which in coyote language
                        meant "to come"
                        and one coyote appeared
                        and he says
                        to this one
                                "Look down below
                                and see the wonder!
                                Look at all that food
                                the *Stro'ro'kas* have brought
                                to give away
                                if one could only get at them."
So the first coyote
was thrilled
and he says
                "How can we get down there?
                The cliff is high and precipitous."
So he said
                "We'll call some others."

230

So the first one
again made a call:
   "Ama doo roo a roo!"
and two more came.
And he said
to the two
who had just arrived
     "Look down below!
      Look what a sight there is!
      All the food
      the *Stro'ro'ka* dancers
      have brought!
      And how can we get
      down there?"
So he said
   "I believe I'll call—
    give another call."
And so he did.
He said
   "Ama doo roo a roo!"
and a whole bunch of them
came—of coyotes.
The first one
said to them
   "Look down below!
    Look what a beautiful sight!

All the food
the *Stro'ro'kas*
and their ceremonial dance
have brought."
and
"How shall we get down there?
So he said
"I think I have an idea.
We know that the cliff
is high
and there's no other way
to get down there,
so I have
an idea."
He says
"I think
if we just hang down
some way—"
He says
"If we just bite
one another's tail
and in that way
we'll go down
in a long string."
So the first one said
"All right
if you'll just bite my tail
I'll lead."

232

And so the second one
bit the leader's tail
and he hung over the cliff.
Do you see the picture?
Yes, they hung over the cliff
and so the third one
bit the second one's tail
and the string got
a little bit longer
and it was over the cliff now
and so on
until there was
a whole group
of the coyotes now
hung down the cliff
until one—
the middle one—
the one in the middle said

         "Oh! I smell a bad odor
          from some source,"
                he said.

And he opened his mouth
and the rest said
        "So do I!"
They let one another go
and the whole bunch
flopped down
in a big heap

in the valley below.
And the *Stro'ro'ka* dancers
down below
stopped dancing
and ran to the heap
of dead coyotes
glad because
they wanted the skins
of the coyotes
to wear around their necks.
And they all grabbed—
the *Stro'ro'ka* dancers grabbed
the dead coyotes
and said
      "This one is going to be mine!"
and "This is going to be
    my neck piece."
And they gathered
the coyotes
and took them.
And tradition says that they—
  the *Stro'ro'ka* Dancers
the mesita people
are the only ones
who dance that now
they wear that costume—
    the coyote skin neckpiece—
  because of long ago.

When the Indian Public Health Service
laid sewer line in the village
the outhouses started disappearing
from the hill next to the church
and from down below by the corrals.
Everyone is happy to quit hauling water in buckets
and everyone enjoys taking showers
so no one discusses this openly.
But I think people are beginning to realize now
the advantages the old outdoor toilets had
especially when pipes freeze in the winter
or the sewer clogs up.
With the outside toilets
you could get away by yourself
for an hour or so
at night you could tell everyone
you were going out to the toilet
and have an hour or two that way.
Many interesting things used to develop.

There are only a few outhouses remaining now
but last year at Laguna Feast
a girl from Encinal was slightly injured.

She had locked herself in one of the old wooden toilets
down by Scotts' pigpen
and she was arguing through the door
with five or six of her boyfriends.
Finally they pushed the toilet down the hill
with her still inside.

The Laguna guys claim it was the Navajos
and the Navajos claim it was the Lagunas who did it.
The girl received a slight scalp wound
as the toilet rolled over.
     "Well she should have held onto the hole!"
       Sandy said when she heard the story,
   "She should have held onto the edge of that hole real tight."

TOE'OSH: A LAGUNA COYOTE STORY

for Simon Ortiz, July 1973

In the wintertime
at night
we tell coyote stories
     and drink Spañada by the stove.
How coyote got his
236 ratty old fur coat

                    bits of old fur
                    the sparrows stuck on him
                    with dabs of pitch.
That was after he lost his proud original one in a poker game.
anyhow, things like that
are always happening to him,
that's what he said, anyway.

And it happened to him at Laguna
and Chinle
and Lukachukai too, because coyote got too smart for his own good.

But the Navajos say he won a contest once.
It was to see who could sleep out in a
snowstorm the longest
and coyote waited until chipmunk badger and skunk were all
curled up under the snow
and then he uncovered himself and slept all night
inside
and before morning he got up and went out again
and waited until the others got up before he came
in to take the prize.

Some white men came to Acoma and Laguna a hundred years ago
and they fought over Acoma land and Laguna women, and even now
some of their descendants are howling in
the hills southeast of Laguna.

Charlie Coyote wanted to be governor
and he said that when he got elected
he would run the other men off
the reservation
and keep all the women for himself.

One year
the politicians got fancy
at Laguna.
They went door to door with hams and turkeys
and they gave them to anyone who promised
to vote for them.
On election day all the people
stayed home and ate turkey
and laughed.

The Trans-Western pipeline vice president came
to discuss right-of-way.
The Lagunas let him wait all day long
because he is a busy and important man.
And late in the afternoon they told him
to come back again tomorrow.

They were after the picnic food
that the special dancers left
down below the cliff.
And Toe'osh and his cousins hung themselves
down over the cliff
holding each other's tail in their mouth making a coyote chain
until someone in the middle farted
and the guy behind him opened his
mouth to say "What stinks?" and they
all went tumbling down, like that.

Howling and roaring
Toe'osh scattered white people
out of bars all over Wisconsin.
He bumped into them at the door
until they said
              "Excuse me"
And the way Simon meant it
was for 300 or maybe 400 years.

Around Laguna Fiesta time
tribal police from everywhere show up: Isleta, Acoma, Zuni,
Navajo Police and of course the Laguna Police invite the
State Police and the B.I.A. Police.
I even saw a few county sheriffs this year.
Anyway, this accounts for all the sirens.

It happened at the trashpile
over by the wooden bridge across the river
where you can't be seen from the road.
Some Navajo guys had planned it very carefully.
They hid their liquor supply in the trash pile
and then went up to the village
for the dances and food stands and carnival.
They would sneak back down to the trash pile for a drink
whenever they wanted.
They were having a wonderful time
until someone noticed them going back and forth
always coming back happier than they went down.

Nobody comes to Laguna Feast
without a six pack and a bottle
but liquor here is still illegal.
Nobody ever pays any attention to the law.
You just pay attention to not getting caught.

They don't usually arrest you
but they take the cold beer away from you
and the worst part is
you know *they'll* drink it.

So when the guys saw all these tribal police cars—
it seemed like every tribe sent a police car—
these guys knew Fiesta was coming to an end for them.
But part of the fiesta spirit
has always been
if not for wine at the trash pile
then for a fight with the cops.

It was a shoving and pushing fight:
the guys shoving the cops away from their liquor
the cops pushing the guys into the paddy wagons.
But carefully
because the tribal police know what the people are saying:
>   It is all these police
>   that have ruined Laguna Feast—
>   not the State Fair going on at the same time.
>   It is because of these police
>   the Navajos don't show up anymore
>   like they once did
>   covering the foothills east and north of Laguna
>   with their campfires.

SKELETON FIXER

What happened here?
she asked
Some kind of accident?
Words like bones
scattered all over the place. . . .

Old Man Badger traveled
from place to place
searching for skeleton bones.
There was something
only he could do with them.

On the smooth sand
Old Man Badger started laying out the bones.
It was a great puzzle for him.
He started with the toes
He loved their curve
like a new moon,
like a white whisker hair.

Without thinking
he knew their direction,
laying each toe bone
to walk east.

242

"I know,
it must have been this way.
Yes,"
he talked to himself as he worked.

He strung the spine bones
as beautiful as any shell necklace.

The leg bones were running
so fast
dust from the ankle joints
surrounded the wind.

"Oh poor dear one who left your bones here
I wonder who you are?"
Old Skeleton Fixer spoke to the bones
Because things don't die
they fall to pieces maybe,
get scattered or separate,
but Old Badger Man can tell
how they once fit together.

Though he didn't recognize the bones
he could not stop;
he loved them anyway.

He took great care with the ribs
marveling at the structure

which had contained the lungs and heart.
Skeleton Fixer had never heard of
such things as souls.
He was certain
only of bones.

But where a heart once beat
there was only sand.
"Oh I will find you one—
somewhere around here!"
And a yellow butterfly
flew up from the grass at his feet.

"Ah! I know how your breath left you—
Like butterflies over an edge,
not falling but fluttering
their wings rainbow colors—
Wherever they are
your heart will be."

He worked all day
He was so careful with this one—
it felt like the most special of all.
   Old Man Badger didn't stop
until the last spine bone
was arranged at the base of the tail.

"A'moo'ooh, my dear one
these words are bones,"
he repeated this
four times
        Pa Pa Pa Pa!
        Pa Pa Pa Pa!
        Pa Pa Pa Pa!
        Pa Pa Pa Pa!

Old Coyote Woman jumped up
and took off running.
She never even said "thanks."

Skeleton Fixer
shook his head slowly.

"It is surprising sometimes," he said
"how these things turn out."
But he never has stopped fixing
the poor scattered bones he finds.

A Piece Of A Bigger Story They Tell Around Laguna and Acoma Too
                    —*From A Version Told by Simon J. Ortiz*

On Sundays Grandpa Hank liked to go driving.
Usually we went to Los Lunas
because Grandma Lillie had relatives there.
We took the old winding road that follows
the San José river until it meets the Rio Puerco.
Not far from the junction of the rivers
is a high prominent mesa of dark volcanic rock.
On one of these Sunday drives long ago
Grandpa told us two of his grand-uncles had died there
killed by the Apaches who stole their sheep.

I remember looking very hard out the window of the car
at the great dark mesa and the rolling plains below it.

I have passed the mesa many times since.
The plains below the mesa
are still as grassy and good range for sheep.
as they had been long ago.

THE STORYTELLER'S ESCAPE

The storyteller keeps the stories
        all the escape stories
                she says "With these stories of ours
                    we can escape almost anything
                    with these stories we will survive."

The old teller has been on every journey
and she knows all the escape stories
        even stories told before she was born.
She keeps the stories for those who return
        but more important
        for the dear ones who do not come back
        so that we may remember them
        and cry for them with the stories.

                    "In this way
                    we hold them
                    and keep them with us forever
                    and in this way
                    we continue."

           This story is remembered
           as her best story
           it is the storyteller's own escape.

———

In those days
the people would leave the village
and hurry into the lava flows
where they waited until the enemy had gone.

"This time they were close behind us
and we could not stop to rest.
On the afternoon of the fourth day
I was wearing the sun
for a hat.

Always before
it was me
turning around
for the last look
at the pregnant woman
the crippled boy
old man Shio'see
slowing up
lying down
never getting up again.

Always before
I was the one who looked back
before the humpback hills
rose between us
so I could tell where these dear ones stopped."

But sooner or later
even a storyteller knows it will happen.
    The only thing was
             this time
             she couldn't be sure
             if there would be anyone
             to look back
             and later tell the others:
                    She stopped on the north side of Dough Mountain
                    and she said:

                        "The sun is a shawl on my back
                         its heat makes tassels that
                         shimmer down my arms."

                    And then she sat down in the shade
                    and closed her eyes.

She was thinking
      this was how she would want them
      to remember her and cry for her
If only somebody had looked back
             to see her face for the last time

      Someone who would know then
                and tell the others:

"The black hills rose between us
the shady rock was above her head
and she was thinking
There won't be any escape story this time
unless maybe someone tells
how the sweat spilled over the rock
making streams in hills
that had no water.

She was thinking
I could die peacefully
if there was just someone to tell
how I finally stopped
and where.

She believed
in this kind of situation
you have to do the best you can.

So I just might as well think of a story
while I'm waiting to die:

A'moo'ooh, the child looked back.

"Don't wait!
Go on without me!
Tell them I said that—
Tell them I'm too old too tired

                                        I'd rather just die here
                                        in the shade
                                        I'd rather just die
                                        than climb these rocky hills
                                        in the hot sun.

The child turned back for a last look at her
off in the distance leaning against a cool rock
the old teller waiting for the enemy to find her.
The child knew
                how she had been on all the escape journeys
                how she hated the enemy.
She knew
            what she was thinking
            what she was saying to herself:

                        "I'll fix them good!
                        I'll fool them!
                        I'll already be dead
                        when the enemies come."

        She laughed out loud.

                        I'll die just to spite them!

She was resting close to the boulder
hoping the child would tell—
otherwise   251

how could they remember her
how could they cry for her
without this story?

About this time
            the sun lifted off from her shoulders like a butterfly.

                              Let the enemy wear it now!
                              Let them see how they like the heat
                              wrapping them in its blanket!

She laughed sitting there
thinking to herself
until it got dark.
                    They would cry when they were told
                    the sun had been her hat
                    until she could walk no more
                    the sun had been a shawl
                    until she had to sit down in the shade.

                              This one's the best one yet—
                              too bad nobody may ever hear it.

She waited all night
but at dawn
there was still no sign of the enemy.
So she decided
to go back to the village.

What difference would it make
if she ran into the enemy?
She had already waited
all night
for them to come along
and finish her.

But she didn't see anyone
no enemy.
Maybe the sun got to be too much for them too

And it was the best escape story she had come up with yet

How four days later when the people came back
from their hide-outs in the lava flow
there she was
sitting in front of her house
waiting for them.

This is the story she told,
the child who looked back,
the old teller's escape—
the story she was thinking of
her getaway story
how they remembered her
and cried for her
Because she always had a way with stories
even on the last day
when she stopped in the shade
on the north side of Dough Mountain.

✗

HELEN'S WARNING AT NEW ORAIBI:

"You must be very quiet and listen respectfully.
Otherwise the storyteller might get upset and pout
and not say another word all night."

✗

In 1918 Franz Boas, ethnologist and linguist
passed through Laguna.
His talented protégé
Elsie Clews Parsons
stayed behind to collect Laguna texts
from which Boas planned to construct
a grammar of the Laguna language.
Boas, as it turns out
was tone-deaf
and the Laguna language is tonal
so it is fortunate he allowed Ms. Parsons
to do the actual collecting of the stories.

Although Boas was never able to construct the Laguna grammar
he did distinguish himself

with the languages of Northwest Coast tribes
which are not tonal languages.

In the collection which Parsons made
there is a coyote story
told in Laguna
by my great-grandfather.
It is a very simple story
with a little song
which is repeated four times
the meadowlark teasing the she-coyote
calling her
              "Coyote long-long-long-long mouth!"
Until Coyote gets so confused and upset
she spits out the water
she was carrying back to her pups.
Four times Coyote tries to carry the water back
and four times Meadowlark sings this song
                           "Coyote long-long-long-long mouth!"
and Coyote opens her mouth
spilling the water.
When she finally gets back to her pups
they are all dead from thirst.

A good deal of controversy surrounded
and still surrounds my great-grandfather and his brother
who both married Laguna women.

Ethnologists blame the Marmon brothers
for all kinds of factions and trouble at Laguna
and I am sure much of it is true—
their arrival was bound to complicate
the already complex politics at Laguna.
They came on the heels of a Baptist preacher named Gorman
who also must have upset Laguna ceremonialism.

All I know of my great-grandpa Marmon
are the stories my family told
and the old photographs which show him
a tall thin old white man
with a white beard
wearing a black suit coat
and derby hat.
He stands with his darker sons
and behind the wire-rim glasses he wore
I see in his eyes
he had come to understand this world
differently.
Maybe he chose that particular coyote story
to tell Parsons
because for him at Laguna
that was the one thing he had to remember:
           No matter what is said to you by anyone
           you must take care of those most dear to you.

He wasn't getting any place with Mrs. Sekakaku, he could see that. She was warming up leftover chili beans for lunch and when her niece came over they left him alone on the red plastic sofa and talked at the kitchen table. Aunt Mamie was still sick that's what her niece was telling her and they were all so worried because the doctors at Keams Canyon said they'd tried everything already and old man Ko'ite had come over from Oraibi and still Aunt Mamie was having dizzy spells and couldn't get out of bed. He was looking at the same *Life* magazine he'd already looked at before and it didn't have any pictures of high school girls twirling batons or plane crashes or anything he wanted to look at more than twice, but he didn't want to listen to them because then he'd know just what kind of gossip Mrs. Sekakaku found more important than him and his visit. He set the magazine down on his lap and traced his finger over the horse head embossed on the plastic cushion. It was always like that. When he didn't expect it, it always came to him, but when he wanted something to happen, like with Mrs. Sekakaku, then it shied away. Mrs. Sekakaku's letters had made the corner of the trading post where the mailboxes were smell like the perfume counter at Woolworth's. The Mexican woman with the fat arms was the postmaster and ran the trading post. She didn't approve of perfumed letters and she used to pretend the letters weren't there even when he could smell them and see their pastel edges sticking out of the pile in the general delivery slot.

The Mexican woman thought Pueblo men were great lovers—he knew this because he heard her say so to another Mexican woman one day while he was finishing his strawberry soda on the other side of the dry goods section. In the summer he spent a good number of hours there watching her because she wore sleeveless blouses that revealed her fat upper arms, full and round, and the tender underarm creases curving to her breasts. They had not noticed he was still there leaning on the counter behind a pile of overalls; ". . . the size of a horse" was all that he had heard, but he knew what she was talking about. They were all like that, those Mexican women. That was all they talked about when they were alone. "As big as a horse"—he knew that much Spanish and more too, but she had never treated him nice, not even when he brought her the heart-shaped box of candy, carried it on the bus

257

all the way from Albuquerque. He didn't think it was being older than her because she was over thirty herself—it was because she didn't approve of men who drank. That was the last thing he did before he left town; he did it because he had to, because liquor was illegal on the reservation. So the last thing he did was have a few drinks to carry home with him the same way other people stocked up on lamb nipples or extra matches. She must have smelled it on his breath when he handed her the candy because she didn't say anything and she left the box under the counter by the old newspapers and balls of string. The cellophane was never opened and the fine gray dust that covered everything in the store finally settled on the pink satin bow. The postmaster was jealous of the letters that were coming, but she was the one who had sent him into the arms of Mrs. Sekakaku.

In her last two letters Mrs. Sekakaku had been hinting around for him to come see her at Bean Dance time. This was after Christmas when he had sent a big poinsettia plant all the way to the Second Mesa on the mail bus. Up until then she had never answered the part in his letters where he said he wished he could see the beautiful Hopi mesas with snow on them. But that had been the first time a potted plant ever

rode into Hopi on the mail bus and Mrs. Sekakaku finally realized the kind of man he was. All along that had been the trouble at Laguna, nobody understood just what kind of man he was. They thought he was sort of good for nothing, he knew that, but for a long time he kept telling himself to keep on trying and trying. But it seemed like people would never forget the time the whole village was called out to clean up for feast day and he sent his mother to tell them he was sick with liver trouble. He was still hurt because they didn't understand that with liver trouble you can walk around and sometimes even ride the bus to Albuquerque. Everyone was jealous of him and they didn't stop to think how much it meant to his mother to have someone living with her in her old age. All they could talk about was the big C.O.D. that came to the post office in his name and she cashed her pension check to pay for it. But she was the one who told him, "Sonny Boy, if you want that jacket, you go ahead and order it." It was made out of brown vinyl resembling leather and he still wore it whenever he went to town. Even on the day she had the last stroke his two older brothers had been telling her to quit paying his bills for him and to make him get out and live on his own. But she always stood up for him in front of the others even if she did complain privately at times to her nieces who then scolded him about the bills from the record club and the correspondence school. He always knew he could be a lawyer—he had listened to the lawyers in the courtrooms of the Federal Building on those hot summer afternoons when he needed a cool place to sit while he waited for the bus to Laguna. He listened and he knew he could be a lawyer because he was so good at making up stories to justify why things happened the way they did. He thought correspondence school would be different from Indian school which had given him stomach aches and made him run away all through his seventh grade year. Right after that he had cut his foot pretty bad chopping wood for his older brother's wife, the one who kept brushing her arm across his shoulders whenever she poured coffee at the supper table. The foot had taken so long to heal that his mother agreed he shouldn't go back to Indian School or chop wood anymore. A few months after that they were all swimming at the river and he hurt his back in a dive off the old wooden bridge so it was no wonder he couldn't do the same work as the other young men.

———

When Mildred told him she was marrying that Hopi, he didn't try to stop her although she stood there for a long time like she was waiting for him to say something. He liked things just the way they were down along the river after dark. Her mother and aunts owned so many fields they expected a husband to hoe and he had already promised his mother he wouldn't leave her alone in her old age. He thought it would be easier this way but after Mildred's wedding, people who had seen him and Mildred together started joking about how he had lost out to a Hopi.

Hopi men were famous for their fast hands and the way they could go on all night. Some of the jokes hinted that he was as lazy at lovemaking as he was with his shovel during Spring ditch cleaning and that he took his girl friends to the deep sand along the river so he could lie on the bottom while they worked on top. But later on, some of the older men took him aside and told him not to feel bad about Mildred and told him about women they'd lost to Hopis when they were all working on the railroad together in Winslow. Women believe those stories about Hopi men, they told him, because women like the sound of those stories, and they don't care if it's the Hopi men who are making up the stories in the first place. So when he finally found himself riding the

259

Greyhound bus into Winslow on his way to see Mrs. Sekakaku and the Bean Dance he got to thinking about those stories about Hopi men. It had been years since Mildred had married that Hopi and her aunts and her mother kept the man working in their fields all year round. Even Laguna people said "poor thing" whenever they saw that Hopi man walking past with a shovel on his shoulder. So he knew he wasn't going because of that—he was going because of Mrs. Sekakaku's letters and because it was lonely living in a place where no one appreciates you even when you keep trying and trying. At Hopi he could get a fresh start; he could tell people about himself while they looked at the photos in the plastic pages of his wallet.

He waited for the mail bus and drank a cup of coffee in the café across the street from the pink stucco motel with a cowboy on its neon sign. He had a feeling something in his life was about to change because of this trip, but he didn't know if it would be good for him or bad. Sometimes he was able to look at what he was doing and to see himself clearly two or three weeks into the future. But this time when he looked, he only saw himself getting off the bus on the sandy shoulder of the highway below Second Mesa. He stared up at the Hopi town on the sandrock and thought that probably he would get married.

The last hundred feet up the wagon trail seemed the greatest distance to him and he felt an unaccustomed tightness in his lungs. He knew it wasn't old age—it was something else—something that wanted him to work for it. A short distance past the outside toilets at the edge of the mesa top he got his breath back and their familiar thick odor reassured him. He saw that one of the old toilets had tipped over and rolled down the side of the mesa to the piles of stove ashes, broken bottles and corn shucks on the slope below. He'd get along all right. Like a lot of people, at one time he believed Hopi magic could outdo all the other Pueblos but now he saw that it was all the same from time to time and place to place. When Hopi men got tired of telling stories about all-nighters in Winslow motels then probably the old men brought it around to magic and how they rigged the Navajo tribal elections one year just by hiding some little painted sticks over near Window Rock. Whatever it was he had come for, he was ready.

He checked his reflection in the window glass of Mrs. Sekakaku's front door before he knocked. Gray hair made him look dignified, that is what she had written after he sent her the photographs. He believed in photographs to show people as you were telling them about yourself and the things you'd done and the places you'd been. He always carried a pocket camera and asked people passing by to snap one of him outside the fancy bars and restaurants in the Heights where he walked after he had a few drinks in the Indian bars downtown. He didn't tell her he'd never been inside those places, that he didn't think Indians were welcome there. Behind him he could hear a dog barking. It sounded like a small dog but it also sounded very upset and little dogs were the first ones to bite. So he turned and at first he thought it was a big rat crawling out the door of Mrs. Sekakaku's bread oven but it was a small gray wire-haired dog that wouldn't step out any further. Only lonely widows let their dogs sleep in the bread oven although they always pretend otherwise and scold the dogs whenever relatives or guests come. It must have known it was about to be replaced because it almost choked on its own barking. "Not much longer little doggy," he was saying softly while he knocked on the door. He was beginning to wonder if she had forgotten he was coming and he could feel his confidence lose its footing just a little. She walked up from behind while he was knocking—something he always dreaded because it made the person knocking look so foolish—knocking and waiting while the one you wanted wasn't inside the house at all but was standing right behind you. The way the little dog was barking probably all the neighbors had seen him and were laughing. He managed to smile and would have shaken hands but she was bending over petting the little dog running around and around her ankles. "I hope you haven't been waiting too long! My poor Aunt Mamie had one of her dizzy spells and I was over helping." She was still looking down at the dog while she said this and he noticed she wasn't wearing her perfume. At first he thought his understanding of the English language must be failing, that really she had only invited him over to Bean Dance, that he had misread her letters when she said that a big house like hers was lonely and that she did not like walking alone in the evenings from the water faucet outside the village. Maybe all this had only meant she was afraid a bunch of Navajos might jump out from the shadows of the mesa rocks to take turns on top of her. But when she warmed up the leftover chili beans and went on talking to her niece about the dizzy spells he began to suspect what was going on. She was one of those kinds of women who wore Evening in Paris to Laguna feast and sprinkled it on letters but back at Hopi she pretended she was somebody else. She had lured his letters and snapshots and the big poinsettia plant to show off to her sisters and aunts, and now his visit so she could pretend he had come uninvited, overcome with desire for her. He should have seen it all along, but the first time he met her at Laguna feast a gust of wind had shown him the little roll of fat above her garter and left him dreaming of a plunge deep into the crease at the edge of the silk stocking. The old auntie and the dizzy spells gave her the perfect excuse and a story to protect her respectability. It was only 2:30 but already she was folding a flannel nightgown while she talked to her niece. And here he had been imagining the night together the whole bus ride from Laguna—fingering the creases and folds and the little rolls while she squeezed him with both hands. Their night to-

gether had suddenly lifted off and up like a butterfly moving away from him, and the breathlessness he had felt coming up the mesa returned. He was feeling bitter—if that's all it took then he'd find a way to get that old woman out of bed. He said it without thinking—the words just found his mouth and he said "excuse me ladies," straightening his belt buckle as he walked across the room, "but it sounds to me like your poor auntie is in bad shape." Mrs. Sekakaku's niece looked at him for the first time all afternoon. "Is he a medicine man?" she asked her aunt and for an instant he could see Mrs. Sekakaku hesitate and he knew he had to say "Yes, it's something I don't usually mention myself. Too many of those guys just talk about it to attract women. But this is a serious case." It was sounding so good that he was afraid he would start thinking about the space between the cheeks of the niece's ass and be unable to go on. But the next thing he said was they had a cure they did at Laguna for dizzy spells like Aunt Mamie was having. He could feel a momentum somewhere inside himself—it wasn't hope, because he knew Mrs. Sekakaku had tricked him—but whatever it was it was going for broke. He imagined the feel of grabbing hold of the tops of the niece's thighs which were almost as fat and would feel almost as good as the tops of Mrs.

Sekakaku's thighs. "There would be no charge. This is something I want to do especially for you." That was all it took because these Hopi ladies were like all the other Pueblo women he ever knew, always worrying about saving money, and nothing made them enemies for longer than selling them the melon or mutton leg they felt they should get for free as a love gift. Because all of them, even the thin ones and the old ones, believed he was after them. "Oh, that would be so kind of you! We are so worried about her!" "Well, not so fast," he said even though his heart was racing. "It won't work unless everything is just so. All her clanswomen must come to her house but there can't be any men there, not even outside." He paused. He knew exactly what to say. "This is very important. Otherwise the cure won't work." Mrs. Sekakaku let out her breath suddenly and tightened her lips and he knew that any men or boys not in the kivas preparing for Bean Dance would be sent far away from Aunt Mamie's house. He looked over at the big loaf of fresh oven bread the niece had brought when she came; they hadn't offered him any before, but now after she served him a big bowl of chili beans she cut him a thick slice. It was all coming back to him now about how good medicine men get treated and he wasn't surprised at himself any-

more. Once he got started he knew just how it should go. It was getting it started that gave him trouble sometimes. Mrs. Sekakaku and her niece hurried out to contact all the women of the Snow Clan to bring them to Aunt Mamie's for the cure. There were so many of them sitting in rows facing the sickbed—on folding chairs and little canvas stools they'd brought just like they did for a kiva ceremony or a summer dance. He had never stopped to think how many Snow Clan women there might be, and as he walked across the room he wondered if he should have made some kind of age limit. Some of the women sitting there were pretty old and bony but then there were all these little girls—one squatted down in front of him to play jacks and he could see the creases and dimples of her legs below her panties. The initiated girls and the women sat serious and quiet with the ceremonial presence the Hopis are famous for. Their eyes were full of the power the clanswomen shared whenever they gathered together. He saw it clearly and he never doubted its strength. Whatever he took, he'd have to run with it, but the women would prevail as they always had.

He sat on the floor by the fireplace and asked them to line up. He reached into the cold white juniper ashes and took a handful and told the

263

woman standing in front of him to raise her skirt above her knees. The ashes were slippery and carried his hands up and around each curve each fold each roll of flesh on her thighs. He reached high but his fingers never strayed above the edge of the panty leg. They stepped in front of him one after the other and he worked painstakingly with each one—the silvery white ashes billowing up like clouds above skin dusted like early snow on brown hills, and he lost all track of time. He closed his eyes so he could feel them better—the folds of skin and flesh above the knee, little crevices and creases like a hawk feels canyons and arroyos while he is soaring. Some thighs he gripped as if they were something wild and fleet like antelope and rabbits, and the women never flinched or hesitated because they believed the recovery of their clansister depended on them. The dimple and pucker at the edge of the garter and silk stocking brought him back, and he gave special attention to Mrs. Sekakaku, the last one before Aunt Mamie. He traced the ledges and slopes with all his fingers pressing in the ashes. He was out of breath and he knew he could not stand up to get to Aunt Mamie's bed so he bowed his head and pretended he was praying. "I feel better already. I'm not dizzy," the old woman said, not letting anyone help her out of bed or walk with her to the fireplace. He rubbed her thighs as carefully as he had rubbed the others, and he could tell by the feel she'd probably live a long time.

The sun was low in the sky and the bus would be stopping for the outgoing mail pretty soon. He was quitting while he was ahead, while the Hopi men were still in the kivas for Bean Dance. He graciously declined any payment but the women insisted they wanted to do something so he unzipped his jacket pocket and brought out his little pocket camera and a flash cube. As many as they could stood with him in front of the fireplace and someone snapped the picture. By the time he left Aunt Mamie's house he had two shopping bags full of pies and piki bread.

Mrs. Sekakaku was acting very different now—when they got back to her house she kicked the little gray dog and blocked up the oven door with an orange crate. But he told her he had to get back to Laguna right away because he had some-thing important to tell the old man. It was some-thing they'd been trying and trying to do for a long time. At sundown the mail bus pulled onto the highway below Second Mesa but he was tast-ing one of the pumpkin pies and forgot to look back. He set aside a fine-looking cherry pie to give to the postmaster. Now that they were even again with the Hopi men maybe this Laguna luck would hold out a little while longer.

24

25

NOTES TO PHOTOGRAPHS

1. Robert G. Marmon with Marie Anaya Marmon, my great-grandparents, holding my grandpa Hank. He was named Henry Anaya Marmon but years later changed his middle name to the initial "C." because at school the kids had teased him for the way his initials spelled out H.A.M. *Photograph: Unknown*

2. When I was a little girl Aunt Susie spent a good deal of time at the Marmon Ranch south of Laguna. At branding time in the summer we used to visit Aunt Susie and Uncle Walter and my father would take pictures of the cattle they rounded up. Aunt Susie used to cook all morning long for the big meal at noontime. *Photograph: Lee H. Marmon*

3. Marie Anaya Marmon, Grandma A'mooh, in her kitchen with my sisters, Wendy and Gigi. *Photograph: Lee H. Marmon*

4. Looking southwest from the sandhills a mile east of Laguna. *Photograph: Lee H. Marmon*

5. Bill Smith was the ranch foreman for the L Bar Cattle company, and he used to let us hunt on Mt. Taylor land the L Bar owned. There was an old cabin there we slept in. My uncle Polly and I have just finished arranging the bucks on the porch of the cabin so they can have their pictures taken. *Photograph: Lee H. Marmon*

6. Looking east from Paguate Village at the open pit uranium mine which the Anaconda company opened on Laguna land in the early 1950's. This photograph was made in the early 1960's. The mesas and hills that appear in the background and the foreground are gone now, swallowed by the mine. In the beginning, the Laguna people did not want the mining done on their land, but then as now, military needs and energy development far outweighed the people. *Photograph: Lee H. Marmon*

7. Looking from the east edge of Laguna village toward the west. *Photograph: Lee H. Marmon*

8. In Laguna Village looking south toward the Chersposy house. *Photograph: Lee H. Marmon*

9. The people believe the cradle board protects a child and when they place the baby on the cradle board, they speak silently to the cradle board, reminding it to take care of the child. My mother kept me on the cradle board until I was twelve months old. *Photograph: Lee H. Marmon*

10. Mr. Kasero and his wife used to drive their wagon and horses up from Mesita village to Laguna to buy groceries and pick up their mail. One time they gave me a ride in their wagon and I remember how wonderfully the rocks and bumps in the road could be felt through the wagon box. Mr. Kasero was especially proud of his corn plants one year and asked my father to photograph them. My father asked

him if he would be in the picture too and Mr. Kasero said okay, as long as the corn plants could be seen. *Photograph: Lee H. Marmon*

11.   Mr. Ottapopie was an Oklahoma Indian minister at the Presbyterian Church at Casa Blanca village, near Laguna. I don't think the Church had much to pay him and Presbyterianism was slowly dying out anyway, but he was always cheerful and busy with his congregation, driving old ladies to their doctor appointments and visiting shut-ins. Every summer he had a vacation bible school at the Casa Blanca church where we made herds of sheep cut out of cotton pasted on colored paper. I don't remember anything about religion—just the crayons and paste and the Kool-Aid they gave us at lunchtime. He spent most of the summer driving us bible students to and from the Church. Georgia Daily and Johnnie Alonzo and I used to bounce up and down on the back seat of his car but he'd just smile. He never knew that we used to make fun of his old car and that the reason my sister Wendy refused to go to bible school was because she didn't want to be seen in his old car. *Photograph: Lee H. Marmon*

12.   A photograph that my Dad took. *Photograph Lee H. Marmon*

13.   The Navajos say the black peaks in this valley are drops of blood that fell from a dying monster which the Twin Brothers fought and fatally wounded. *Photograph: Lee H. Marmon*

14.   Navajo wagons at Laguna Fiesta in the early 1950's. *Photograph: Lee H. Marmon*

15.   Kat'sima, Enchanted Mesa. *Photograph: Lee H. Marmon*

16. My father learned photography while he was in the Army during the Second World War. Some of his best work he did with the Speed Graphic. *Photograph: Virginia L. Hampton*

17. For a while in the late 1920's my great-grandpa Stagner ran a cafe at Laguna. There was also a camp ground there and a few motel cabins but after cars started going faster and U. S. Route 66 was paved, tourists and travellers no longer needed to stop at Laguna. *Photograph: Henry C. Marmon*

18. My sisters with the buck my father brought back one hunting season. *Photograph: Lee H. Marmon*

19. Grandpa Hank. *Photograph: Lee H. Marmon*

20. Grandpa Hank and his 1933 Auburn. *Photograph: Henry C. Marmon*

21. Grandma A'mooh. *Photograph: Lee H. Marmon*

22. The Laguna Regulars in 1928, 43 years after they rode in the Apache Wars. *Photograph: Unknown*

23. Looking southwest from Idle Hour Ranch at Wasson Peak, the highest point in the Tucson Mountains, Arizona. *Photograph: Denny Carr*

26

24. In the Cottonwood Wash below Wasson Peak in the Tucson Mountains, Arizona. *Photograph: Denny Carr*

25. On the right is my grandpa Hank after he returned from Sherman Institute and began working for Abie Abraham in his store, and on the left, Arthur Abraham, Abie's brother. *Photograph: Unknown*

26. With Pa'toe'ch Mesa visible at the extreme left of the photograph are Uncle Kenneth, Grandpa Hank's brother, my great-grandpa Robert G. Marmon, Charlie Pierce who married Aunt Bess, Grandpa Hank's sister, and Uncle Walter, Grandpa Hank's brother. The two little boys are my father, Lee Marmon, and my uncle Polly, Richard H. Marmon. *Photograph: Henry C. Marmon*

CONTENTS

There is a tall Hopi basket with a single figure   1

I always called her Aunt Susie   3

Aunt Susie had certain phrases   7

My great-grandmother was Marie Anaya   16

Storyteller   17

It was a long time before   33

Indian Song: Survival   35

The Laguna People   38

Lullaby   43

Grandma Lillie was born in Los Lunas, New Mexico   52

What Whirlwind Man Told Kochininako, Yellow Woman   54

Yellow Woman   54

Cottonwood: Parts One & Two   63

The Time We Climbed Snake Mountain   76

When I was thirteen I carried an old .30-30   77

Aunt Alice told my sisters and me this story one time   82

Grandpa Stagner had a wagon and team and water drilling rig   88

His wife had caught them together before   89

Grandma A'mooh had a worn-out little book   93

Storytelling   94

The Two Sisters   100

Out of the Works No Good Comes From   103

Saturday morning I was walking past Nora's house   110

One time   111

Poem for Myself and Mei: Concerning Abortion   122

Tony's Story   123

Long time ago   130

Estoy-eh-muut and the Kunideeyahs   140

The go-wa-peu-zi song   158

It was summertime   158

The hills and mesas around Laguna   160

Up North   161

The purple asters are growing   170

Simon J. Ortiz is a wonderful poet   170

Uncle Tony's Goat   171

How to Write a Poem about the Sky   177

In Cold Storm Light   178

Prayer to the Pacific   179

Horses at Valley Store   181

September 20, the day after Laguna Feast   182

The Man to Send Rain Clouds   182

Many of the Navajo people   187

Deer Dance/For Your Return   188

Grandpa graduated from Sherman Institute   192

A Hunting Story for my grandpa, H.C. Marmon   193

Grandpa Hank had grown up mostly at Paguate   197

Where Mountain Lion Lay Down with Deer   199

Deer Song   200

At Laguna Feast time   202

Preparations   203

Story from Bear Country   204

He was a small child   207

Grandma A'mooh used to tell me stories   210

It seems like a good idea   210

A Geronimo Story   212

I just fed the rooster a blackened banana (from a letter)   226

Coyotes and the Stro'ro'ka Dancers   229

When the Indian Public Health Service   235

Toe'Osh: A Laguna Coyote Story for Simon Ortiz, July 1973   236

Around Laguna Fiesta time   240

Skeleton Fixer   242

On Sundays Grandpa Hank liked to go driving   246

The Storyteller's Escape   247

Helen's Warning at New Oraibi   254

In 1918 Franz Boas, ethnologist and linguist   254

Coyote Holds a Full House in his Hand   257

Notes to Photographs   269